IoT Development With Python And JavaScript

A Comprehensive Guide To Designing, Building
And Deploying Innovative IoT Solutions, From
Prototyping To Production

Bronson E. Lee

Table Of Content

DISCLAIMER

The authors and publishers of "IoT Development With Python And JavaScript" have diligently striven to ensure the accuracy and completeness of the information contained within this book at the time of publication. However, it is crucial to acknowledge that the field of software development, including IoT Development, is characterized by rapid advancements and evolving best practices.

Therefore, the authors and publishers offer no warranty, express or implied, regarding the enduring accuracy, completeness, suitability, or effectiveness of the information presented herein. Readers are strongly encouraged to remain abreast of the latest developments in IoT Development, associated technologies, and industry best practices through continued learning and engagement with relevant resources.

The authors and publishers shall not be held liable for any errors, omissions, or any losses or damages of any kind arising from the use of, or reliance upon, the information contained within this book. This includes, but is not limited to, incidental, consequential, or punitive damages.

The code examples provided in this book are intended for illustrative purposes only and may necessitate modification to suit specific applications or environments. The reader assumes full responsibility for the implementation and consequences of utilizing any code, techniques, or methodologies described herein.

All trademarks, trade names, and logos mentioned in this book are the property of their respective owners. Any references to third-party resources, websites, or materials are provided for convenience and informational purposes only. The authors and publishers do not endorse or assume any responsibility for the content, accuracy, or availability of such external resources.

By utilizing the information presented in this book, the reader acknowledges and agrees to the terms of this disclaimer.

INTRODUCTION

The world around us is undergoing a profound transformation. Everyday objects, from the mundane to the extraordinary, are gaining intelligence and connectivity, blurring the lines between the physical and digital realms. This revolution is fueled by the **Internet of Things (IoT)**, a vast network of devices embedded with technology that allows them to communicate, interact, and exchange data.

This book, **IoT Development with Python and JavaScript**, invites you to embark on a journey into this exciting landscape, equipping you with the skills and knowledge to design, build, and deploy innovative IoT solutions. Whether you're a seasoned developer or a curious beginner, this book will guide you through the fundamentals and advanced concepts of IoT, empowering you to create impactful applications that address real-world challenges.

Why Python and JavaScript?

We've chosen Python and JavaScript as the languages of choice for this book due to their versatility, extensive libraries, and strong community support. Python, with its clear syntax and powerful data processing capabilities, excels in back-end development, data analysis, and machine learning. JavaScript, the language of the web, shines in front-end development, real-time communication, and interactive user interfaces. By combining the strengths of both languages, you can create comprehensive IoT solutions that are both powerful and user-friendly.

What You'll Learn

This book takes a comprehensive approach to IoT development, covering a wide range of topics, including:

- **Fundamentals of IoT:** Understand the core concepts, architecture, and applications of IoT.
- **Hardware and Software:** Explore popular microcontrollers like Raspberry Pi, Arduino, and ESP32, and learn to use essential software tools and libraries.
- **Communication Protocols:** Master communication protocols like MQTT, HTTP, and CoAP for seamless data exchange.
- **Data Handling:** Learn to represent, store, and manage IoT data using formats like JSON and XML.

- **Security:** Implement security measures to protect your devices and data from threats and vulnerabilities.
- **Data Analytics and Visualization:** Extract insights from your IoT data using basic data analysis techniques and create compelling visualizations.
- **Edge Computing:** Explore the concepts and benefits of edge computing and learn to deploy AI and ML models at the edge.
- **Advanced Topics:** Delve into advanced topics like LPWAN, scalability, and reliability.
- **Real-World Projects:** Build practical IoT projects, including a home automation system, an environmental monitoring system, and a smart agriculture system.

Who This Book Is For

This book is designed for a wide range of readers, including:

- **Software developers:** Expand your skills into the realm of IoT and build connected applications.
- **Hardware enthusiasts:** Learn to program microcontrollers and integrate them into IoT solutions.

- **Students and hobbyists:** Gain a practical understanding of IoT concepts and build exciting projects.
- **Professionals in various industries:** Explore how IoT can transform your field and create innovative solutions.

A Journey of Learning and Discovery

This book is more than just a technical guide; it's an invitation to explore the vast possibilities of the Internet of Things. As you progress through the chapters, you'll gain the knowledge and confidence to build your own IoT solutions, contributing to a world where technology seamlessly integrates with our lives.

So, let's embark on this journey of learning and discovery, together. Turn the page and step into the fascinating world of connected things.

Chapter I. Introduction to the Internet of Things

What is IoT? Definitions, Concepts, and Applications

Our world is undergoing a profound transformation, where everyday objects are gaining intelligence and connectivity, blurring the lines between the physical and digital realms. This revolution is fueled by the **Internet of Things (IoT)**, a vast network of devices embedded with technology that allows them to communicate and interact with each other and their environment. This chapter provides a foundational understanding of IoT, its key concepts, and its transformative impact across diverse industries.

Defining the Internet of Things

Imagine a refrigerator that automatically orders groceries when supplies dwindle, a car that self-diagnoses mechanical issues, or a home that intelligently adjusts lighting and temperature based on your preferences. These scenarios, once confined to science fiction, are becoming reality thanks to the Internet of Things.

At its essence, IoT connects ordinary objects to the internet, empowering them to exchange information and perform actions based on the data they gather. This interconnectedness enables a new level of automation, efficiency, and insight across various domains.

Core attributes of IoT devices include:

- **Sensing and Actuation:** Embedded sensors and actuators enable these devices to perceive and respond to their surroundings. Sensors collect data such as temperature, humidity, pressure, and motion, while actuators trigger actions like switching devices on/off, adjusting settings, or controlling mechanical components.
- **Network Connectivity:** IoT devices leverage various communication technologies, including Wi-Fi, Bluetooth, cellular networks, and specialized IoT protocols like MQTT and CoAP, to connect to the internet and exchange data with other devices and systems.
- **Data Processing:** Many IoT devices possess onboard processing capabilities, allowing them to perform basic data analysis and decision-making. More complex processing can be offloaded to the cloud or edge devices.

- **Intelligence and Automation:** By combining data from multiple sources and applying intelligent algorithms, IoT systems can automate tasks, optimize processes, and provide valuable insights.

Essential Concepts and Terminology

Navigating the world of IoT requires understanding its core concepts and terminology:

- **Things:** These are the physical objects connected to the internet, ranging from simple sensors and wearables to complex industrial machines and vehicles.
- **Data:** The lifeblood of IoT, data is generated by sensors, processed by devices and systems, and used to trigger actions, generate insights, and improve decision-making.
- **Connectivity:** This encompasses the diverse technologies and protocols that enable communication between IoT devices and other systems, including the internet, cloud platforms, and edge devices.
- **Cloud Computing:** Cloud platforms provide the infrastructure and services for storing,

processing, and analyzing the massive amounts of data generated by IoT devices.

- **Edge Computing:** Processing data closer to the source (on the device or a nearby gateway) to reduce latency, conserve bandwidth, and enable real-time responsiveness.
- **Security:** Safeguarding IoT devices and data from unauthorized access, cyberattacks, and data breaches is paramount to ensure the integrity and reliability of IoT systems.

The Expanding Realm of IoT Applications

The potential applications of IoT are vast and continue to expand as technology evolves. Here are some prominent examples:

- **Smart Homes:** Automating lighting, heating, security systems, and appliances to enhance comfort, convenience, and energy efficiency.
- **Wearable Technology:** Tracking fitness metrics, monitoring health conditions, and providing personalized insights to promote well-being.
- **Industrial Automation:** Optimizing manufacturing processes, supply chain

management, and logistics to improve efficiency, productivity, and safety.

- **Smart Cities:** Enhancing urban living through intelligent traffic management, environmental monitoring, and resource optimization.
- **Precision Agriculture:** Utilizing sensors and data analytics to monitor crop health, optimize irrigation, and improve yields in agriculture.
- **Healthcare:** Revolutionizing healthcare with remote patient monitoring, smart medical devices, and data-driven diagnostics.
- **Environmental Monitoring:** Tracking air quality, water levels, and other environmental factors to support sustainability and conservation efforts.

These examples merely scratch the surface of IoT's transformative potential. As technology advances, we can anticipate even more innovative and impactful applications to emerge.

The Synergy of Python and JavaScript in IoT

Python and JavaScript are two dominant programming languages in the IoT landscape. Python, renowned for its clear syntax and extensive libraries, excels in data analysis, machine learning, and back-end development. JavaScript, on the other hand, is well-suited for front-end development, web interfaces, and real-time communication.

By harnessing the strengths of both languages, developers can create robust and versatile IoT solutions. Python can handle the complexities of data processing and analysis, while JavaScript enables seamless user interfaces and efficient communication between devices and users.

This book will guide you through the fundamentals of IoT development using Python and JavaScript, equipping you with the skills and knowledge to design, build, and deploy innovative IoT solutions.

The IoT Ecosystem: Devices, Networks, and Platforms

The Internet of Things is more than just connected devices; it's a complex ecosystem of interconnected components working together to collect, process, and exchange data. Understanding this ecosystem is crucial for navigating the world of IoT and building effective solutions. This section explores the key elements that comprise the IoT ecosystem: devices, networks, and platforms.

Devices: The "Things" in IoT

At the heart of the IoT ecosystem lie the **devices**, or "things," that gather data and interact with the physical world. These devices can be broadly categorized into three types:

- **Sensors:** These devices detect and measure physical phenomena like temperature, humidity, pressure, light, motion, and sound. They convert these measurements into digital data that can be processed and analyzed. Examples include thermometers, accelerometers, GPS modules, and cameras.
- **Actuators:** These devices perform actions in the physical world based on commands or data received from other devices or systems. Examples include motors, solenoids, relays, and displays.
- **Gateways:** These devices act as intermediaries between sensors, actuators, and other devices, facilitating communication and data exchange. They often perform tasks like data aggregation, protocol translation, and edge computing.

IoT devices come in various shapes and sizes, ranging from tiny sensors embedded in clothing to large industrial machines. The choice of device depends on the specific application and the type of data being collected or the action being performed.

Networks: Connecting the Dots

Networks provide the essential infrastructure for communication and data exchange within the IoT ecosystem. They enable devices to connect to each other, to the internet, and to cloud platforms. A variety of network technologies are used in IoT, each with its own strengths and weaknesses:

- **Short-range networks:** These networks are suitable for connecting devices within a limited area, such as a home or office. Examples include:
  - **Wi-Fi:** Widely used for its high bandwidth and ease of use.
  - **Bluetooth:** Low-power technology ideal for connecting wearables and other small devices.
  - **Zigbee:** A mesh network protocol designed for low-power, low-data rate applications.
  - **Z-Wave:** Another mesh network protocol commonly used in home automation.

- **Wide-area networks (WANs):** These networks cover larger geographical areas and are used to connect devices across cities, countries, or even continents. Examples include:
    - **Cellular networks (3G, 4G, 5G):** Provide widespread coverage and high bandwidth, but can be expensive for high-data applications.
    - **Low-Power Wide-Area Networks (LPWANs):** Designed for long-range, low-power communication, making them ideal for applications like environmental monitoring and smart agriculture. Examples include LoRaWAN, Sigfox, and NB-IoT.

The choice of network technology depends on factors like range, bandwidth requirements, power consumption, and cost.

Platforms: Managing and Analyzing IoT Data

Platforms provide the software and services that enable the management, processing, and analysis of data generated by IoT devices. They act as the central hub for the IoT ecosystem, connecting devices, networks, and applications. Key functionalities of IoT platforms include:

- **Device management:** Provisioning, configuring, and monitoring IoT devices.
- **Data ingestion:** Collecting, storing, and processing data from devices.
- **Data analysis:** Applying analytics and machine learning algorithms to extract insights from data.
- **Application enablement:** Providing tools and APIs for developing IoT applications.
- **Security:** Implementing security measures to protect devices, data, and the platform itself.

Several leading cloud providers offer comprehensive IoT platforms, including:

- **AWS IoT:** Amazon Web Services' IoT platform, providing a wide range of services for device management, data ingestion, analytics, and application development.
- **Azure IoT Hub:** Microsoft Azure's IoT platform, offering similar functionalities to AWS IoT with a focus on integration with other Azure services.
- **Google Cloud IoT Core:** Google Cloud Platform's IoT platform, known for its scalability and strong data analytics capabilities.

In addition to these cloud-based platforms, there are also open-source platforms and platforms designed for specific industries or applications.

Understanding the interplay between devices, networks, and platforms is essential for designing, building, and deploying effective IoT solutions. By carefully selecting the right components and integrating them seamlessly, you can create IoT systems that deliver valuable insights and transform businesses and industries.

Why Python and JavaScript for IoT?

In the vast landscape of programming languages, Python and JavaScript stand out as powerful tools for IoT development. Each language brings its own strengths to the table, making them a compelling combination for building diverse and innovative IoT solutions. This section explores the reasons why Python and JavaScript are particularly well-suited for IoT, highlighting their individual advantages and how they complement each other in this domain.

Python: The Versatile Backbone

Python has gained immense popularity in various fields, including data science, machine learning, and web development. Its versatility extends to IoT, where it shines in several key areas:

- **Readability and Ease of Use:** Python's clear and concise syntax makes it easy to learn and use, even for beginners. This is particularly beneficial in IoT, where developers often need to work with complex hardware and software systems.
- **Extensive Libraries and Frameworks:** Python boasts a rich ecosystem of libraries and frameworks specifically designed for[1] IoT development. These libraries simplify tasks like interacting with sensors and actuators, communicating with cloud platforms, and performing data analysis. Some popular libraries include:
  - `RPi.GPIO`: For controlling GPIO pins on Raspberry Pi.
  - `smbus2`: For communicating with I2C devices.
  - `paho-mqtt`: For implementing MQTT communication.
  - `requests`: For making HTTP requests to web services.
-
- **Data Science and Machine Learning Capabilities:** Python is a leading language

for data science and machine learning, making it ideal for analyzing IoT data and building intelligent applications. Libraries like NumPy, Pandas, and Scikit-learn provide powerful tools for data manipulation, analysis, and machine learning.[2]

- **Strong Community Support:** Python has a large and active community of developers, providing ample resources, tutorials, and support for IoT projects. This vibrant community ensures that you can find help and guidance whenever you need it.

JavaScript: The Front-End and Real-Time Powerhouse

JavaScript, the language of the web, also plays a crucial role in IoT development. Its strengths lie in:

- **Front-End Development:** JavaScript is the go-to language for building interactive and dynamic web interfaces. In IoT, this is essential for creating user-friendly dashboards, visualizations, and control panels for managing and monitoring devices.
- **Real-Time Communication:** JavaScript excels at handling real-time communication, which is critical for many IoT applications.

Technologies like WebSockets enable seamless bidirectional communication between devices and web applications, allowing for instant updates and responsive interactions.

- **Node.js for Server-Side Development:** Node.js, a JavaScript runtime environment, allows developers to use JavaScript for server-side development. This enables the creation of scalable and efficient IoT applications that can handle large amounts of data and concurrent connections.
- **Wide Adoption in Web Development:** JavaScript's ubiquity in web development makes it a natural choice for building IoT applications that integrate with existing web infrastructure.

The Synergistic Duo

While Python and JavaScript each have their own strengths, they truly shine when used together in IoT projects. Python can handle the back-end tasks, such as data processing, analysis, and communication with devices and cloud platforms. JavaScript can then be used to create the front-end interfaces that allow users to interact with the system and visualize data in a meaningful way.

This synergy enables the development of comprehensive IoT solutions that are both powerful and user-friendly. For example, Python can be used to collect and analyze data from sensors, while JavaScript can create a dynamic dashboard that displays the data in real-time and allows users to control devices remotely.

By combining the versatility of Python with the front-end and real-time capabilities of JavaScript, you can unlock the full potential of IoT and build innovative solutions that address real-world challenges.

Chapter II. Setting Up Your IoT Development Environment

Essential Hardware: Microcontrollers (Raspberry Pi, Arduino, ESP32/ESP8266)

Embarking on your IoT development journey requires a well-equipped workspace. This chapter focuses on the essential hardware components that form the foundation of your IoT projects: microcontrollers. We'll delve into the characteristics, strengths, and applications of three popular choices: Raspberry Pi, Arduino, and ESP32/ESP8266.

Understanding Microcontrollers

Microcontrollers are compact, integrated circuits that serve as the brains of embedded systems. They combine a processor core, memory, and input/output peripherals on a single chip, enabling them to control and interact with their environment. In the context of IoT, microcontrollers play a pivotal role in collecting data from sensors, processing information, and controlling actuators.

Raspberry Pi: A Versatile Computing Platform

The Raspberry Pi is a credit-card-sized single-board computer that has revolutionized the world of computing and DIY electronics. Initially designed to promote computer science education, it has become a popular choice for hobbyists, makers, and professionals alike.

Key Features:

- **Powerful Processor:** Raspberry Pi models feature ARM-based processors, ranging from modest to quite powerful, capable of running a full-fledged operating system like Linux.
- **Ample Memory and Storage:** Raspberry Pi boards come equipped with generous RAM (typically 1GB to 8GB) and support various storage options, including microSD cards and USB drives.
- **Versatile Connectivity:** Raspberry Pi offers a wide range of connectivity options, including Wi-Fi, Bluetooth, Ethernet, USB ports, and GPIO (General Purpose Input/Output) pins for interfacing with sensors and actuators.
- **Large and Active Community:** The Raspberry Pi enjoys a massive and enthusiastic community of users and

developers, providing a wealth of resources, tutorials, and support.

Why Choose Raspberry Pi for IoT?

- **Full Operating System:** The ability to run a full operating system like Linux allows for greater flexibility and the use of powerful software tools.
- **Versatility:** Raspberry Pi can handle a wide range of tasks, from simple data logging to complex machine learning applications.
- **Ease of Use:** The Raspberry Pi Foundation provides excellent documentation and resources, making it easy to get started.

Popular Raspberry Pi Models:

- **Raspberry Pi 4 Model B:** The flagship model, offering a powerful quad-core processor, ample RAM, and Gigabit Ethernet.
- **Raspberry Pi Pico:** A microcontroller-class board based on the RP2040 chip, offering a cost-effective option for simpler projects.

Arduino: The Accessible Prototyping Platform

Arduino is an open-source electronics platform based on easy-to-use hardware and software. It's a favorite among beginners and makers for its simplicity and accessibility.

Key Features:

- **Simplified Programming:** Arduino uses a simplified version of C++, making it easier to learn than traditional programming languages.
- **Arduino IDE:** The Arduino IDE provides a user-friendly environment for writing, uploading, and testing code.
- **Large Selection of Boards:** Arduino offers a wide variety of boards with different features and capabilities, catering to various project needs.
- **Extensive Shield Ecosystem:** "Shields" are add-on boards that expand the functionality of Arduino boards by providing features like motor control, GPS, and networking.

Why Choose Arduino for IoT?

- **Beginner-Friendly:** Arduino's simplicity and ease of use make it an ideal platform for learning the basics of electronics and programming.

- **Large Community:** Arduino has a vast and supportive community, offering a wealth of resources and tutorials.
- **Cost-Effective:** Arduino boards are relatively inexpensive, making them accessible to hobbyists and students.

Popular Arduino Boards:

- **Arduino Uno:** The most popular Arduino board, offering a good balance of features and ease of use.
- **Arduino Nano:** A compact version of the Uno, suitable for projects with limited space.
- **Arduino Mega:** A more powerful board with more memory and I/O pins.

ESP32/ESP8266: Wi-Fi Enabled Microcontrollers

The ESP32 and ESP8266 are low-cost, Wi-Fi enabled microcontrollers that have gained immense popularity in the IoT space. They offer a compelling combination of features, performance, and affordability.

Key Features:

- **Integrated Wi-Fi:** Both ESP32 and ESP8266 have built-in Wi-Fi capabilities, making it easy to connect to the internet.
- **Low Power Consumption:** These microcontrollers are designed for low-power operation, making them suitable for battery-powered applications.
- **Arduino Compatibility:** Both ESP32 and ESP8266 can be programmed using the Arduino IDE, leveraging the familiar Arduino ecosystem.
- **Affordable:** These microcontrollers are incredibly cost-effective, making them an attractive option for hobbyists and makers.

Why Choose ESP32/ESP8266 for IoT?

- **Built-in Wi-Fi:** Simplifies connecting to the internet and building networked applications.
- **Low Cost:** Makes them an accessible option for a wide range of projects.
- **Arduino Compatibility:** Allows developers to leverage the Arduino ecosystem and existing libraries.

Choosing the Right Microcontroller

The choice of microcontroller depends on the specific requirements of your IoT project. Consider factors like processing power, memory, connectivity options, power consumption, and cost when making your decision.

- **For complex projects requiring a full operating system and ample processing power, Raspberry Pi is an excellent choice.**
- **For simpler projects, prototyping, and learning the basics of electronics, Arduino offers an accessible and user-friendly platform.**
- **For projects requiring Wi-Fi connectivity and low power consumption, ESP32 and ESP8266 are compelling options.**

By understanding the strengths and limitations of each microcontroller, you can select the best tool for your IoT endeavors.

Software Tools: Python, Node.js, IDEs, and Libraries

Having explored the essential hardware components, let's now turn our attention to the software tools that will empower you to write code, build applications, and bring your IoT projects to life. This section covers the key software elements you'll need in your IoT development journey: programming languages (Python and JavaScript),

Integrated Development Environments (IDEs), and essential libraries.

Python: The Language of Versatility

Python has become a cornerstone of IoT development, thanks to its readability, extensive libraries, and strong community support. It's a versatile language that can handle a wide range of tasks, from basic scripting to complex data analysis and machine learning.

Key Aspects for IoT:

- **Clear Syntax:** Python's straightforward syntax makes it easy to learn and use, even for those new to programming. This reduces the learning curve and allows you to focus on building your IoT projects.
- **Rich Libraries:** Python offers a vast collection of libraries specifically designed for IoT development. These libraries simplify tasks like:
    - **Hardware Interaction:** `RPi.GPIO` (for Raspberry Pi), `smbus2` (for I2C communication)
    - **Networking:** `socket`, `requests`
    - **Data Processing:** `NumPy`, `Pandas`

- **Machine Learning:** `Scikit-learn, TensorFlow`
- **Cross-Platform Compatibility:** Python runs on various operating systems, including Windows, macOS, and Linux, providing flexibility in your development environment.

JavaScript: Empowering the Web and Beyond

JavaScript, the language of the web, plays a crucial role in IoT, particularly in front-end development and real-time communication.

Key Aspects for IoT:

- **Front-End Development:** JavaScript is essential for building interactive web interfaces for your IoT applications. This includes creating dashboards, visualizations, and control panels for managing and monitoring devices.
- **Real-Time Communication:** JavaScript, with technologies like WebSockets, enables seamless real-time communication between devices and web applications. This is crucial for applications requiring instant updates and responsive interactions.
- **Node.js:** Node.js, a JavaScript runtime environment, extends JavaScript's

capabilities to the server-side. This allows you to build scalable and efficient IoT applications that can handle large amounts of data and concurrent connections.

Integrated Development Environments (IDEs)

IDEs provide a comprehensive environment for writing, testing, and debugging code. They offer features like syntax highlighting, code completion, and debugging tools that streamline the development process.

Popular IDEs for IoT:

- **Visual Studio Code (VS Code):** A lightweight yet powerful IDE with excellent support for Python and JavaScript. It offers a wide range of extensions for IoT development, making it a versatile choice.
- **Thonny:** A beginner-friendly IDE specifically designed for Python, making it a great option for those new to the language.
- **Atom:** Another popular open-source IDE with good support for Python and JavaScript. It's highly customizable and offers a wide range of packages for various development needs.

- **PyCharm:** A professional IDE for Python development with advanced features like code analysis and refactoring tools. It's a good choice for larger projects and experienced developers.

Essential Libraries

Libraries are pre-written code modules that provide ready-to-use functionalities, saving you time and effort in your development process. Here are some essential libraries for IoT development with Python and JavaScript:

Python Libraries:

- **RPi.GPIO:** For controlling GPIO pins on Raspberry Pi.
- **smbus2:** For communicating with I2C devices.
- **paho-mqtt:** For implementing MQTT communication.
- **requests:** For making HTTP requests to web services.
- **NumPy:** For numerical computing and data manipulation.
- **Pandas:** For data analysis and manipulation.

JavaScript Libraries:

- **Socket.IO:** For real-time, bidirectional communication.
- **Express.js:** A popular web framework for Node.js.
- **MQTT.js:** A client library for MQTT communication.
- **Chart.js:** For creating data visualizations.

By mastering these software tools, you'll be well-equipped to tackle a wide range of IoT projects, from simple prototypes to complex, real-world applications. Remember that the best tools for your project will depend on your specific needs and preferences. Explore different options and choose the ones that best suit your development style and project requirements.

Connecting to the Cloud: AWS IoT, Azure IoT Hub, Google Cloud IoT Core

While microcontrollers provide the intelligence and processing power for IoT devices, and networks facilitate communication, the cloud plays a crucial role in enabling scalability, data storage, and advanced analytics. This section explores three leading cloud platforms for IoT: AWS IoT, Azure IoT Hub, and Google Cloud IoT Core (though now deprecated, it's still valuable to understand its concepts as they apply to other platforms).

Cloud Computing in IoT: Expanding the Horizons

Cloud computing provides on-demand access to a shared pool of computing resources, including servers, storage, databases, and[1] software, over the internet. In the context of IoT, cloud platforms offer a range of benefits:

- **Scalability:** Cloud platforms can handle massive amounts of data generated by millions of devices, allowing your IoT solutions to grow without constraints.
- **Data Storage and Management:** Cloud storage provides a secure and reliable repository for your IoT data, enabling you to store, manage, and access data from anywhere.
- **Advanced Analytics:** Cloud platforms offer powerful analytics tools and machine learning services that can extract valuable insights from your IoT data.
- **Reduced Infrastructure Costs:** By leveraging cloud resources, you can avoid the upfront costs and maintenance associated with building and managing your own infrastructure.

AWS IoT: A Comprehensive Suite of Services

Amazon Web Services (AWS) offers a comprehensive suite of IoT services, with AWS IoT Core at its center.

Key Features:

- **Device Management:** Securely connect, monitor, and manage millions of devices.
- **Data Ingestion and Processing:** Ingest data from devices, process it in real-time, and store it for analysis.
- **Analytics and Machine Learning:** Utilize AWS analytics services like Amazon Kinesis and Amazon SageMaker to gain insights from your IoT data.
- **Security:** Secure your IoT infrastructure with features like device authentication, data encryption, and access control.
- **Integration with other AWS Services:** Seamlessly integrate with other AWS services like Amazon S3, Amazon DynamoDB, and AWS Lambda.

Azure IoT Hub: A Scalable Messaging Platform

Microsoft Azure's IoT Hub is a cloud-hosted message broker that connects millions of devices to Azure cloud services.

Key Features:

- **Bi-directional Communication:** Enables secure, reliable communication between devices and the cloud.
- **Device Management:** Register, organize, and monitor your IoT devices.
- **Scalability:** Handles massive amounts of data and millions of concurrent connections.
- **Security:** Provides robust security features like device authentication and data encryption.
- **Integration with other Azure Services:** Integrates with other Azure services like Azure Stream Analytics, Azure Machine Learning, and Azure Cosmos DB.

Google Cloud IoT Core: (Deprecated) A Foundation for Connected Devices

While Google Cloud IoT Core is no longer available, it's worth understanding its core concepts as they are fundamental to many IoT cloud platforms.

Key Features (as it existed):

- **Device Manager:** Provided secure device connection and management.
- **Protocol Bridges:** Supported MQTT and HTTP protocols for device communication.
- **Data Ingestion:** Integrated with Google Cloud Pub/Sub for scalable data ingestion.
- **Integration with Google Cloud Services:** Connected with other Google Cloud services like BigQuery for data analytics and Cloud Functions for serverless computing.

Choosing the Right Cloud Platform

The choice of cloud platform depends on your specific needs and preferences. Consider factors like:

- **Existing Infrastructure:** If you already use AWS, Azure, or Google Cloud Platform for other services, it might be beneficial to choose their corresponding IoT platform for easier integration.
- **Features and Services:** Evaluate the features and services offered by each platform and choose the one that best aligns with your requirements.

- **Pricing:** Compare the pricing models of each platform and choose the most cost-effective option for your needs.
- **Community and Support:** Consider the size and activity of the community and the level of support offered by each platform.

By connecting your IoT devices to the cloud, you can unlock the full potential of your IoT solutions, enabling scalability, advanced analytics, and seamless integration with other cloud services.

Chapter III. Programming for IoT with Python

Python Basics for IoT: Data Types, Control Flow, Functions

Python's clarity and versatility make it an ideal language for diving into the world of IoT programming. This chapter lays the groundwork by introducing the fundamental building blocks of Python: data types, control flow, and functions. Mastering these concepts will equip you with the essential skills to write effective Python code for your IoT projects.

Data Types: The Building Blocks of Information

In Python, data types define the kind of values a variable can hold and the operations that can be performed on it. Understanding data types is crucial for writing correct and efficient code. Here are some essential data types in Python:

- **Numeric Types:**
    - **Integers (`int`):** Whole numbers, e.g., `10, -5, 0`.

- **Floating-Point Numbers** (`float`): Numbers with decimal points, e.g., `3.14, -2.5, 0.0`.
- **Text Type:**
  - **Strings** (`str`): Sequences of characters enclosed in single or double quotes, e.g., `"Hello"`, `'Python'`.
- **Boolean Type:**
  - **Booleans** (`bool`): Represent truth values, either `True` or `False`. Used in logical operations and conditional statements.
- **Sequence Types:**
  - **Lists** (`list`): Ordered collections of items, mutable (can be changed), e.g., `[1, 2, 'apple']`.
  - **Tuples** (`tuple`): Ordered collections of items, immutable (cannot be changed after creation), e.g., `(1, 2, 'apple')`.
- **Mapping Type:**
  - **Dictionaries** (`dict`): Collections of key-value pairs, e.g., `{'name': 'John', 'age': 30}`.

Understanding these data types and how to use them is essential for manipulating and processing data in your IoT applications. For instance, you might use integers to store sensor readings, strings to represent device names, and lists to store multiple data points.

Control Flow: Directing the Program's Execution

Control flow statements determine the order in which code is executed. They allow you to introduce logic and decision-making into your programs.

- **Conditional Statements:**
  - `if` **statement:** Executes a block of code if a condition is true.
  - `elif` **statement:** (Optional) Executes a block of code if the previous condition is false and this condition is true.
  - `else` **statement:** (Optional) Executes a block of code if all previous conditions are false.

Python

```
temperature = 25
if temperature > 30:
```

```
print("It's hot!")
elif temperature > 20:
    print("It's warm.")
else:
    print("It's cool.")
```

- **Loops:**
  - ○ `for` **loop:** Iterates over a sequence (e.g., a list or a string).
  - ○ `while` **loop:** Repeats a block of code as long as a condition is true.

Python

```
# for loop
for i in range(5):
    print(i)  # Prints 0, 1, 2, 3, 4

# while loop
count = 0
while count < 5:
    print(count)
    count += 1
```

Control flow statements are crucial for creating dynamic IoT applications that respond to changing conditions. For example, you might use an `if` statement to trigger an action if a sensor reading exceeds a certain threshold, or a `for` loop to process a series of data points.

Functions: Organizing Your Code

Functions are reusable blocks of code that perform specific tasks. They help you organize your code, make it more modular, and avoid repetition.

- **Defining a Function:**

Python

```python
def greet(name):
    """This function greets the person
passed in as a parameter."""
    print(f"Hello, {name}!")

greet("Alice")  # Output: Hello, Alice!
```

- **Calling a Function:** Once defined, you can call a function by its name, passing any required arguments.
- **Returning Values:** Functions can return values using the `return` statement.

Python

```python
def add(x, y):
    """This function adds two numbers and returns the sum."""
    return x + y

result = add(5, 3)  # result will be 8
```

In IoT development, functions can be used to encapsulate tasks like reading sensor data, controlling actuators, or sending data to the cloud. This makes your code more organized, reusable, and easier to maintain.

By understanding these core Python concepts – data types, control flow, and functions – you'll be well-equipped to write effective and efficient code for your IoT projects.

Interfacing with Sensors and Actuators using Python

Now that we've covered the basics of Python, it's time to explore how to use this powerful language to interact with the physical world through sensors and actuators. This section delves into the practical aspects of interfacing with these essential components, enabling your IoT devices to sense their environment and take action.

Sensors: Gathering Data from the Real World

Sensors are the eyes and ears of your IoT devices, capturing data about the physical world and converting it into digital signals that can be processed by your microcontroller. There's a vast array of sensors available, each designed to measure a specific physical phenomenon.

Common Sensor Types:

- **Temperature Sensors:** Measure temperature in Celsius or Fahrenheit. Examples include:
    - **DHT11/DHT22:** Measure temperature and humidity.
    - **DS18B20:** Digital temperature sensor with high accuracy.

- ○ **Thermocouples:** Measure a wide range of temperatures.
- **Light Sensors:** Detect the intensity of light. Examples include:
  - ○ **Photoresistors:** Resistance changes with light intensity.
  - ○ **Photodiodes:** Generate current proportional to light intensity.
- **Motion Sensors:** Detect movement or changes in position. Examples include:
  - ○ **PIR Sensors:** Detect infrared radiation from moving objects.
  - ○ **Ultrasonic Sensors:** Measure distance using sound waves.
  - ○ **Accelerometers:** Measure acceleration and tilt.
- **Pressure Sensors:** Measure pressure in various units (e.g., Pascals, PSI). Examples include:
  - ○ **BMP180/BMP280:** Measure barometric pressure and altitude.
  - ○ **Piezoresistive Pressure Sensors:** Resistance changes with applied pressure.
- **Gas Sensors:** Detect the presence of specific gases. Examples include:

- MQ-series Gas Sensors: Detect various gases like carbon monoxide, methane, and smoke.

Actuators: Taking Action in the Physical World

Actuators are the muscles of your IoT devices, enabling them to interact with and manipulate their environment based on the data received from sensors or user input.

Common Actuator Types:

- **Motors:** Convert electrical energy into mechanical motion. Examples include:
  - **DC Motors:** Rotate continuously in one direction.
  - **Servo Motors:** Rotate to a specific angle.
  - **Stepper Motors:** Rotate in discrete steps.
- **Relays:** Electromechanical switches that can control high-voltage circuits with a low-voltage signal.
- **Solenoids:** Electromagnetic devices that convert electrical energy into linear motion.
- **LEDs (Light-Emitting Diodes):** Emit light when current passes through them.

- **Buzzers and Speakers:** Produce sound based on electrical signals

Interfacing with Sensors and Actuators using Python

Python provides libraries and tools that simplify the process of interfacing with sensors and actuators. Here's a general workflow:

1. **Connect the Sensor/Actuator:** Connect the sensor or actuator to your microcontroller's GPIO pins, following the wiring diagram provided in the device's documentation.
2. **Install Necessary Libraries:** Install the Python libraries required to interact with the specific sensor or actuator. For example, to use a DHT11 temperature and humidity sensor, you might install the `Adafruit_DHT` library.
3. **Write Python Code:** Write Python code to:
   - **Initialize the sensor/actuator:** Configure the device and set any necessary parameters.
   - **Read data from the sensor:** Use library functions to read data from the sensor and store it in variables.

- Process the data: Perform any necessary calculations or conversions on the sensor data.
- Control the actuator: Use library functions to send commands to the actuator based on the sensor data or user input.

Example: Reading Temperature and Humidity with DHT11

Python

```python
import Adafruit_DHT

# Set sensor type and GPIO pin
sensor = Adafruit_DHT.DHT11
pin = 4

# Read data from the sensor
humidity,          temperature          =
Adafruit_DHT.read_retry(sensor, pin)

# Check if reading was successful
if humidity is not None and temperature is
not None:
        print(f'Temp={temperature:.1f}*C¹
Humidity={humidity:.1f}%')
else:
      print('Failed to get reading. Try
again!')
```

This code snippet demonstrates how to use the `Adafruit_DHT` library to read temperature and humidity data from a DHT11 sensor connected to GPIO pin 4.

By combining your knowledge of Python with the ability to interface with sensors and actuators, you can create IoT devices that gather data from the real world and take action based on that data. This opens up a world of possibilities for building innovative and impactful IoT solutions.

Building IoT Applications with Python Libraries (RPi.GPIO, smbus2)

As we go deeper into Python for IoT, we'll explore two powerful libraries that significantly simplify the process of interacting with hardware components: `RPi.GPIO` and `smbus2`. These libraries provide the necessary functions and abstractions to control GPIO pins, communicate with I2C devices, and ultimately bridge the gap between your Python code and the physical world.

RPi.GPIO: Controlling GPIO Pins on Raspberry Pi

The `RPi.GPIO` library is specifically designed for controlling the General Purpose Input/Output (GPIO) pins on Raspberry Pi. These pins provide a digital interface for interacting with a wide range of electronic components, including sensors, actuators, and displays.

Key Functionalities:

- **Pin Modes:** Configure GPIO pins as inputs or outputs.
  - **Input Mode:** Read digital signals from sensors or buttons.
  - **Output Mode:** Send digital signals to control LEDs, relays, or other actuators.
- **Reading Input Values:** Read the current state of an input pin (HIGH or LOW).
- **Setting Output Values:** Set the state of an output pin (HIGH or LOW) to turn devices on or off.
- **PWM (Pulse-Width Modulation):** Generate PWM signals to control the brightness of LEDs or the speed of motors.

- **Event Detection:** Detect changes in the state of input pins (e.g., rising edge, falling edge) to trigger actions.

Example: Controlling an LED

Python

```python
import RPi.GPIO as GPIO
import time

# Set GPIO numbering mode
GPIO.setmode(GPIO.BCM)

# Set pin 17 as output
led_pin = 17
GPIO.setup(led_pin, GPIO.OUT)

# Blink the LED
try:
    while True:
        GPIO.output(led_pin, GPIO.HIGH)   # Turn LED on
        time.sleep(1)                     # Wait for 1 second
        GPIO.output(led_pin, GPIO.LOW)    # Turn LED off
        time.sleep(1)                     # Wait for 1 second
finally:
```

```
    GPIO.cleanup()    # Clean up GPIO pins on
exit
```

This code snippet demonstrates how to use `RPi.GPIO` to control an LED connected to GPIO pin 17. The LED blinks on and off with a 1-second interval.

smbus2: Communicating with I2C Devices

I2C (Inter-Integrated Circuit) is a popular communication protocol used to connect microcontrollers to various peripheral devices, such as sensors, displays, and real-time clocks. The `smbus2` library provides a Python interface for communicating with I2C devices.

Key Functionalities:

- **I2C Bus Access:** Open and access the I2C bus on your Raspberry Pi.
- **Reading and Writing Data:** Read data from and write data to I2C devices.
- **SMBus Functionality:** Supports SMBus (System Management Bus) commands for

advanced communication with compatible devices.

Example: Reading Data from an I2C Temperature Sensor

Python

```python
import smbus2
import bme280  # Assuming you have a BME280 sensor

# I2C bus number and device address
port = 1
address = 0x76  # BME280 default address

# Create an I2C bus object
bus = smbus2.SMBus(port)

# Initialize the BME280 sensor
calibration_params                              =
bme280.load_calibration_params(bus,
address)

# Read data from the sensor
data    =    bme280.sample(bus,    address,
calibration_params)

# Print the temperature, pressure, and
humidity
print(f"Temperature: {data.temperature:.2f}
°C")
print(f"Pressure: {data.pressure:.2f} hPa")
```

```
print(f"Humidity: {data.humidity:.2f} %")
```

This example shows how to use smbus2 to read data from a BME280 temperature, pressure, and humidity sensor connected to the I2C bus.

Combining Libraries for Powerful Applications

By combining RPi.GPIO and smbus2, you can create sophisticated IoT applications that interact with a wide range of sensors and actuators. For example, you could use smbus2 to read temperature data from a sensor and then use RPi.GPIO to control a fan based on the temperature reading.

These libraries, along with the core Python concepts we've covered, provide a solid foundation for building diverse and innovative IoT projects. As you progress, you can explore other Python libraries and frameworks to further expand your capabilities and tackle more complex challenges.

Chapter IV. Programming for IoT with JavaScript

JavaScript Basics for IoT: Variables, Operators, Functions, Objects

While Python excels in back-end processing and data analysis, JavaScript takes center stage when it comes to building interactive user interfaces and enabling real-time communication in IoT applications. This chapter introduces the fundamental building blocks of JavaScript: variables, operators, functions, and objects. Mastering these concepts will empower you to write effective JavaScript code for your IoT projects.

Variables: Storing and Managing Data

Variables are like containers that hold data in your JavaScript code. They allow you to store information, such as sensor readings, user input, or configuration settings, and manipulate it throughout your program.

- **Declaring Variables:**
    - Use the `var`, `let`, or `const` keywords to declare variables.

- var is the older way to declare variables (with function scope).
- let allows you to reassign values to variables (with block scope).
- const is used for variables whose values should not change after initialization (with block scope).

JavaScript

```
var message = "Hello, IoT!";
let temperature = 25;
const pi = 3.14159;
```

- **Naming Variables:**
    - Choose descriptive names that indicate the purpose of the variable.
    - Use camelCase notation (e.g., sensorReading, deviceName).
- **Data Types:**
    - JavaScript is dynamically typed, meaning you don't need to explicitly specify the data type of a variable. Common data types include:
        - **Number:** For numeric values (e.g., 10, 3.14).

- **String:** For text (e.g., `"Hello"`, `'JavaScript'`).
- **Boolean:** For true/false values (`true` or `false`).
- **Object:** For complex data structures (more on this later).
- **Array:** For ordered collections of items (e.g., `[1, 2, 3]`).
- **Null:** Represents the intentional absence of a value.
- **Undefined:** Indicates that a variable has not been assigned a value.

Operators: Performing Actions on Data

Operators allow you to perform actions on data, such as arithmetic calculations, comparisons, and logical operations.

- **Arithmetic Operators:**
    - `+` (addition), `-` (subtraction), `*` (multiplication), `/` (division), `%` (modulo).
-
- **Comparison Operators:**
    - `==` (equal to), `!=` (not equal to), `>` (greater than), `<` (less[1] than), `>=`

(greater than or equal to), `<=` (less than or equal to).

-
- **Logical Operators:**
  - `&&` (logical AND), `||` (logical OR), `!` (logical NOT).

-
- **Assignment Operators:**[2]
  - `=` (assignment), `+=` (add and assign), `-=` (subtract and assign), etc.

JavaScript

```
let x = 10;
let y = 5;
let sum = x + y;   // sum will be 15
let isEqual = x == y;   // isEqual will be
false
```

Functions: Reusable Blocks of Code

Functions are reusable blocks of code that perform specific tasks. They help you organize your code, make it more modular, and avoid repetition.

- **Defining a Function:**

JavaScript

```
function greet(name) {
  console.log("Hello, " + name + "!");
}

greet("Alice");  // Output: Hello, Alice!
```

- **Calling a Function:** Once defined, you can call a function by its name, passing any required arguments.
- **Returning Values:** Functions can return values using the `return` statement.

JavaScript

```
function add(x, y) {
  return x + y;
}

let result = add(5, 3);  // result will be
8
```

In IoT development, functions can be used to encapsulate tasks like reading sensor data, processing data, sending data to the cloud, or controlling actuators.

Objects: Representing Complex Data

Objects allow you to represent complex data structures in JavaScript. They are collections of key-value pairs, where the keys are strings (or symbols) and the values can be of any data type.

- **Creating Objects:**

JavaScript

```javascript
let device = {
  name: "My IoT Device",
  status: "online",
  temperature: 25,
  sendTelemetry: function() {
    // Code to send telemetry data
  }
};
```

- **Accessing Object Properties:** You can access object properties using dot notation (e.g., device.name) or bracket notation (e.g., device["status"]).

Objects are useful for representing IoT devices, sensor readings, or configuration settings. For instance, you could create an object to represent a smart thermostat, with properties like `currentTemperature`, `targetTemperature`, and `mode`.

By mastering these core JavaScript concepts – variables, operators, functions, and objects – you'll be well-prepared to write effective and efficient code for your IoT projects.

Node.js for IoT: Event Loop, Modules, Asynchronous Programming

As we continue our exploration of JavaScript for IoT, we'll delve into Node.js, a powerful JavaScript runtime environment that extends JavaScript's capabilities beyond the web browser. This section focuses on key Node.js concepts: the event loop, modules, and asynchronous programming. Understanding these concepts is crucial for building efficient and scalable IoT applications with Node.js.

Node.js: JavaScript Beyond the Browser

Node.js allows you to execute JavaScript code outside of a web browser, making it ideal for server-side applications, command-line tools, and, of course, IoT development. It provides a rich set of built-in modules and APIs for interacting with the operating system, networking, and file systems.

The Event Loop: The Heart of Node.js

Node.js operates on a single-threaded event loop model. This means that it can handle multiple concurrent requests without creating multiple threads, making it highly efficient and scalable.

How the Event Loop Works:

1. **Event Queue:** When a request is received (e.g., a network request, a file read), it's placed in an event queue.
2. **Event Loop:** The event loop continuously monitors the event queue. When it finds an event, it picks it up and processes it.
3. **Non-Blocking Operations:** For time-consuming operations (e.g., network requests), Node.js uses non-blocking I/O. Instead of waiting for the operation to complete, it registers a callback function and continues processing other events.
4. **Callback Execution:** When the time-consuming operation finishes, it notifies the event loop, which then executes the associated callback function.

This event-driven, non-blocking approach allows Node.js to handle many concurrent connections without blocking the execution of other tasks, making it ideal for real-time IoT applications.

Modules: Organizing Your Code

Modules in Node.js help you organize your code into reusable units. They encapsulate related functionality and allow you to import and use code from other modules.

- **Creating Modules:**
    - Create a JavaScript file (e.g., `myModule.js`) and define functions or variables you want to export.
    - Use the `module.exports` object to specify what you want to make available to other modules.

JavaScript

```
// myModule.js
function greet(name) {
  console.log("Hello, " + name + "!");
}

module.exports = { greet };
```

- **Using Modules:**
    - o Use the `require()` function to import a module into your code.

JavaScript

```
// main.js
const myModule = require('./myModule');

myModule.greet("Alice");   // Output: Hello, Alice!
```

Modules promote code reusability and maintainability, making it easier to manage complex IoT projects.

Asynchronous Programming: Handling Non-Blocking Operations

Asynchronous programming is essential in Node.js to avoid blocking the event loop while performing time-consuming operations. Node.js provides several mechanisms for asynchronous programming:

- **Callbacks:** Functions that are executed after an asynchronous operation completes.
- **Promises:** Objects that represent the eventual result of an asynchronous operation.
- **Async/Await:** Syntactic sugar that makes asynchronous code look and behave a bit more like synchronous code.

Example: Reading a File Asynchronously

JavaScript

```javascript
const fs = require('fs');

fs.readFile('myFile.txt', 'utf8', (err, data) => {
  if (err) {
    console.error("Failed to read the file:", err);
    return;
  }
  console.log("File contents:", data);
});

console.log("This will be printed before the file contents.");
```

In this example, `fs.readFile()` reads the file asynchronously. The callback function is executed when the file reading is complete. Notice how the last `console.log()` statement is executed before the file contents are printed, demonstrating the non-blocking nature of Node.js.

By understanding the event loop, modules, and asynchronous programming, you can leverage the full power of Node.js to build efficient, scalable, and real-time IoT applications.

Building Web Interfaces for IoT Devices with JavaScript

In the realm of IoT, where user interaction and data visualization are paramount, JavaScript's prowess in web development truly shines. This section explores how to leverage JavaScript's capabilities to create engaging and informative web interfaces for your IoT devices. These interfaces will serve as the bridge between your users and the connected world, enabling them to monitor data, control devices, and gain insights from their IoT systems.

The Role of Web Interfaces in IoT

Web interfaces provide a user-friendly way to interact with IoT devices and systems. They can be accessed from any device with a web browser, be it a desktop computer, laptop, tablet, or smartphone. In the context of IoT, web interfaces serve several key purposes:

- **Data Visualization:** Present sensor data in a clear and meaningful way through charts, graphs, and dashboards.
- **Device Control:** Allow users to remotely control and manage their IoT devices.
- **System Monitoring:** Provide real-time insights into the status and performance of IoT systems.
- **User Interaction:** Enable users to interact with their IoT devices through forms, buttons, and other interactive elements.

Essential Technologies

Building web interfaces for IoT involves a combination of front-end and back-end technologies.

Front-end Technologies:

- **HTML:** Provides the structure and content of the web page.
- **CSS:** Styles the appearance of the web page.

- **JavaScript:** Adds interactivity and dynamic behavior to the web page.
- **JavaScript Libraries and Frameworks:** Simplify web development with pre-built components and functionalities. Popular choices include:
    - **React:** A component-based library for building user interfaces.
    - **Angular:** A full-fledged framework for building complex web applications.
    - **Vue.js:** A progressive framework for building user interfaces.
    - **Chart.js:** For creating data visualizations.

Back-end Technologies:

- **Node.js:** Provides a runtime environment for executing JavaScript on the server-side.
- **Express.js:** A popular web framework for Node.js that simplifies web application development.
- **WebSockets:** Enables real-time, bidirectional communication between the web interface and the IoT devices.

Building a Simple Web Interface

Let's illustrate the process with a basic example of a web interface that displays temperature readings from an IoT device.

1. Set up the Back-end:

- Use Node.js and Express.js to create a web server.
- Implement an API endpoint that retrieves temperature data from your IoT device (e.g., via MQTT or HTTP).
- Use WebSockets to push real-time temperature updates to the web interface.

2. Create the Front-end:

- Use HTML to create the structure of the web page, including a container to display the temperature reading.
- Use CSS to style the appearance of the web page.
- Use JavaScript to:
  - Connect to the WebSocket server.
  - Receive temperature updates from the server.
  - Update the temperature reading on the web page dynamically.

Example Code Snippet (Front-end):

JavaScript

```javascript
// Connect to the WebSocket server
const          socket         =          new
WebSocket('ws://your-server-address');

// Receive temperature updates
socket.onmessage = function(event) {
          const          temperature          =
JSON.parse(event.data).temperature;

document.getElementById('temperature').text
Content = temperature;
};
```

This code snippet demonstrates how to connect to a WebSocket server and update the content of an HTML element with the ID "temperature" whenever a new temperature reading is received.

Enhancing the User Experience

To create truly engaging web interfaces, consider these additional elements:

- **Interactive Charts and Graphs:** Use libraries like Chart.js to visualize data in a more compelling way.

74

- **User Controls:** Add buttons, sliders, and other input elements to allow users to control their IoT devices.
- **Responsive Design:** Ensure your web interface adapts to different screen sizes and devices.
- **User Authentication:** Implement authentication mechanisms to secure access to your IoT system.

By combining your knowledge of JavaScript, Node.js, and front-end technologies, you can build powerful and user-friendly web interfaces that enhance the value and usability of your IoT solutions.

Chapter V. Communication Protocols for IoT

The Internet of Things thrives on the seamless flow of information between devices, applications, and the cloud. This intricate dance of data exchange is orchestrated by communication protocols, each designed with specific strengths and characteristics. This chapter delves into MQTT (Message Queuing Telemetry Transport), a lightweight and efficient protocol that has become a cornerstone of IoT communication.

MQTT: A Lightweight Champion for IoT

MQTT is a publish/subscribe messaging protocol that excels in resource-constrained environments, making it a perfect fit for the often limited bandwidth and processing power of IoT devices. It's designed for efficient and reliable communication, even over unreliable networks, ensuring that your IoT data reaches its destination.

Key Characteristics of MQTT:

- **Lightweight:** MQTT has a small code footprint and minimal overhead, making it ideal for resource-constrained devices.
- **Publish/Subscribe Model:** This model decouples the sender (publisher) from the receiver (subscriber), allowing for flexible and scalable communication.
- **Quality of Service (QoS):** MQTT offers different levels of QoS to ensure message delivery reliability based on application needs.
- **Data Agnostic:** MQTT can transport any type of data, from simple sensor readings to complex JSON payloads.
- **Suitable for Unreliable Networks:** MQTT is designed to handle intermittent connections and network disruptions, making it robust for IoT deployments.

The Publish/Subscribe Model

MQTT's publish/subscribe model is a key differentiator from traditional request/response protocols. In this model, senders (publishers) publish messages to topics, which are essentially named channels. Receivers (subscribers) subscribe to topics of interest and receive messages published to those topics.

Key Players:

- **Publisher:** Sends messages to a specific topic.
- **Subscriber:** Receives messages from topics it has subscribed to.
- **Broker:** An intermediary server that manages the distribution of messages between publishers and subscribers.

Benefits of Publish/Subscribe:

- **Decoupling:** Publishers and subscribers don't need to know about each other, promoting flexibility and scalability.
- **Efficiency:** The broker handles message routing, reducing the overhead on individual devices.
- **Flexibility:** Subscribers can subscribe to multiple topics, and publishers can publish to multiple topics.

Quality of Service (QoS) Levels

MQTT offers three levels of Quality of Service to ensure message delivery reliability:

- **QoS 0 (At most once):** The message is delivered at most once, with no guarantee of delivery. Suitable for applications where occasional message loss is acceptable.

- **QoS 1 (At least once):** The message is delivered at least once, ensuring that it reaches the subscriber. There might be duplicate messages.
- **QoS 2 (Exactly once):** The message is delivered exactly once, ensuring both delivery and no duplicates. This provides the highest level of reliability.

MQTT in Action: An Example

Let's illustrate MQTT with a simple example of a temperature sensor publishing readings to a topic:

1. **The sensor (publisher) connects to an MQTT broker.**
2. **The sensor publishes temperature readings to a topic (e.g., "sensor/temperature").**
3. **A web application (subscriber) subscribes to the "sensor/temperature" topic.**
4. **Whenever the sensor publishes a new reading, the broker forwards it to the web application.**

This demonstrates how MQTT enables seamless communication between an IoT device and an application, even if they are geographically separated and connected through an unreliable network.

MQTT Libraries and Tools

Several libraries and tools are available to simplify MQTT implementation in your IoT projects:

- **Paho MQTT:** A popular open-source MQTT client library available for various programming languages, including Python and JavaScript.
- **Mosquitto:** A lightweight and widely used open-source MQTT broker.
- **MQTT.js:** A JavaScript library for MQTT communication, particularly useful for web-based IoT applications.

By understanding the core concepts of MQTT and utilizing available libraries, you can effectively integrate this powerful protocol into your IoT solutions, enabling efficient and reliable communication between your devices, applications, and the cloud.

HTTP and REST APIs for IoT Data Exchange

While MQTT excels in lightweight, publish/subscribe messaging, HTTP (Hypertext Transfer Protocol) and REST (Representational State Transfer) APIs offer a different approach to IoT data exchange. Rooted in the foundations of the web, HTTP and REST provide a familiar and versatile framework for connecting IoT devices, applications, and services. This section explores how these technologies facilitate data exchange in the IoT landscape.

HTTP: The Foundation of the Web

HTTP is the underlying protocol that powers the World Wide Web. It's a request/response protocol where clients (e.g., web browsers, IoT devices) send requests to servers, and servers respond with the requested data or actions.

Key Characteristics of HTTP:

- **Request/Response Model:** Clients initiate communication by sending requests to servers. Servers process the requests and send back responses.

- **Stateless:** Each request is independent of previous requests, making HTTP simple and scalable.
- **Versatile:** HTTP can transport various types of data, including text, images, videos, and JSON.
- **Ubiquitous:** HTTP is supported by virtually all internet-connected devices, making it a widely accessible protocol.

REST APIs: A Standardized Approach

REST, or Representational State Transfer, is an architectural style that leverages HTTP to create web services. REST APIs define a set of constraints and principles for designing web services that are scalable, interoperable, and easy to use.

Key Principles of REST:

- **Client-Server Architecture:** Separates concerns between clients and servers, promoting modularity and scalability.
- **Statelessness:** Each request from the client to the server must contain all the information necessary to understand the request.

- **Cacheability:** Responses from the server should explicitly state whether they can be cached or not, improving performance.
- **Uniform Interface:** Defines a consistent way to interact with resources using standard HTTP methods (GET, POST, PUT, DELETE).
- **Layered System:** Allows for intermediaries (e.g., load balancers, caches) to be introduced between the client and server without affecting their interaction.

HTTP and REST in IoT

HTTP and REST APIs are widely used in IoT for various purposes:

- **Data Collection:** IoT devices can send sensor data to web servers using HTTP POST requests.
- **Device Control:** Web applications can send commands to IoT devices using HTTP PUT or POST requests.
- **Data Retrieval:** Applications can retrieve data from IoT devices using HTTP GET requests.
- **Cloud Integration:** Cloud platforms often expose REST APIs for interacting with IoT devices and services.

Example: Sending Sensor Data to a Server

An IoT device with a temperature sensor can send data to a web server using an HTTP POST request with a JSON payload:

JSON

```
{
  "deviceId": "device123",
  "temperature": 25.5
}
```

The server can then process this data, store it in a database, or trigger actions based on the received information.

Benefits of HTTP and REST in IoT

- **Simplicity and Familiarity:** HTTP and REST are well-established technologies with a large developer community and extensive resources.
- **Interoperability:** REST APIs promote interoperability between different systems and platforms.

- **Scalability:** HTTP and REST are designed for scalability, making them suitable for large IoT deployments.
- **Web Integration:** Seamlessly integrates with existing web infrastructure and technologies.

By understanding the capabilities of HTTP and REST APIs, you can leverage these powerful tools to build robust and scalable IoT solutions that seamlessly exchange data between devices, applications, and the cloud.

CoAP: Constrained Application Protocol for IoT

While MQTT excels in lightweight, publish/subscribe messaging, HTTP (Hypertext Transfer Protocol) and REST (Representational State Transfer) APIs offer a different approach to IoT data exchange. Rooted in the foundations of the web, HTTP and REST provide a familiar and versatile framework for connecting IoT devices, applications, and services. This section explores how these technologies facilitate data exchange in the IoT landscape.

HTTP: The Foundation of the Web

HTTP is the underlying protocol that powers the World Wide Web. It's a request/response protocol where clients (e.g., web browsers, IoT devices) send requests to servers, and servers respond with the requested data or actions.

Key Characteristics of HTTP:

- **Request/Response Model:** Clients initiate communication by sending requests to servers. Servers process the requests and send back responses.
- **Stateless:** Each request is independent of previous requests, making HTTP simple and scalable.
- **Versatile:** HTTP can transport various types of data, including text, images, videos, and JSON.
- **Ubiquitous:** HTTP is supported by virtually all internet-connected devices, making it a widely accessible protocol.

REST APIs: A Standardized Approach

REST, or Representational State Transfer, is an architectural style that leverages HTTP to create web services. REST APIs define a set of constraints and principles for designing web services that are scalable, interoperable, and easy to use.

Key Principles of REST:

- **Client-Server Architecture:** Separates concerns between clients and servers, promoting modularity and scalability.
- **Statelessness:** Each request from the client to the server must contain all the information necessary to understand the request.[1]
- **Cacheability:** Responses from the server should explicitly state whether they can be cached or not, improving performance.
- **Uniform Interface:** Defines a consistent way to interact with resources using standard HTTP methods (GET, POST, PUT, DELETE).
- **Layered System:** Allows for intermediaries (e.g., load balancers, caches) to be introduced between the client and server without affecting their interaction.

HTTP and REST in IoT

HTTP and REST APIs are widely used in IoT for various purposes:

- **Data Collection:** IoT devices can send sensor data to web servers using HTTP POST requests.
- **Device Control:** Web applications can send commands to IoT devices using HTTP PUT or POST requests.
- **Data Retrieval:** Applications can retrieve data from IoT devices using HTTP GET requests.
- **Cloud Integration:** Cloud platforms often expose REST APIs for interacting with IoT devices and services.

Example: Sending Sensor Data to a Server

An IoT device with a temperature sensor can send data to a web server using an HTTP POST request with a JSON payload:

JSON

```
{
  "deviceId": "device123",
  "temperature": 25.5
}
```

The server can then process this data, store it in a database, or trigger actions based on the received information.

Benefits of HTTP and REST in IoT

- **Simplicity and Familiarity:** HTTP and REST are well-established technologies with a large developer community and extensive resources.
- **Interoperability:** REST APIs promote interoperability between different systems and platforms.
- **Scalability:** HTTP and REST are designed for scalability, making them suitable for large IoT deployments.
- **Web Integration:** Seamlessly integrates with existing web infrastructure and technologies.

By understanding the capabilities of HTTP and REST APIs, you can leverage these powerful tools to build robust and scalable IoT solutions that seamlessly exchange data between devices, applications, and the cloud.

Chapter VI. Data Formats and Data Handling in IoT

JSON and XML for IoT Data Representation

In the interconnected world of IoT, data is the lifeblood that fuels insights, automation, and decision-making. This data, generated by myriad sensors and devices, needs to be structured and organized in a way that facilitates efficient exchange and processing. This chapter explores two prominent data formats that play a crucial role in IoT data representation: JSON and XML. We'll delve into their structures, strengths, and how they are used to represent information within IoT systems.

JSON (JavaScript Object Notation)

JSON has emerged as a dominant data format in web development and IoT, favored for its simplicity, readability, and compatibility with JavaScript. It's a lightweight text-based format that represents data as key-value pairs, arrays, and nested objects, making it ideal for representing structured information.

Structure of JSON:

- **Key-Value Pairs:** Data is represented as key-value pairs, where the key is a string enclosed in double quotes, and the value can be a string, number, boolean, array, object, or null.

JSON

```
{
  "deviceId": "device123",
  "temperature": 25.5
}
```

- **Arrays:** Ordered lists of values enclosed in square brackets.

JSON

```
{
  "sensorReadings": [25.5, 26.2, 25.8]
}
```

- **Nested Objects:** Objects can be nested within other objects to represent hierarchical data structures.

JSON

```
{
  "device": {
    "id": "device123",
    "location": "living room",
    "sensors": {
      "temperature": 25.5,
      "humidity": 60
    }
  }
}
```

Strengths of JSON in IoT:

- **Lightweight:** JSON's concise syntax reduces data size, making it efficient for transmission over networks, especially in bandwidth-constrained IoT environments.
- **Readability:** JSON's simple structure is easy for both humans and machines to read

and understand, facilitating debugging and data analysis.

- **JavaScript Compatibility:** JSON is natively supported by JavaScript, making it easy to parse and manipulate in web applications and Node.js environments.
- **Wide Adoption:** JSON is widely used in web APIs and data exchange, making it a versatile choice for IoT integration.

XML (Extensible Markup Language)

XML is a markup language that defines a set of rules for encoding documents in a format that is both human-readable and machine-readable. It uses tags to define elements and attributes to provide additional information about those elements.

Structure of XML:

- **Elements:** Defined by start and end tags, e.g., `<temperature>25.5</temperature>`.
- **Attributes:** Provide additional information about elements, e.g., `<sensor id="sensor123">`.

- **Nested Elements:** Elements can be nested within other elements to create hierarchical structures.

XML

```
<device id="device123">
  <location>living room</location>
  <sensors>
    <temperature>25.5</temperature>
    <humidity>60</humidity>
  </sensors>
</device>
```

Strengths of XML in IoT:

- **Extensibility:** XML allows you to define your own tags and structures, making it adaptable to various data representation needs.
- **Data Validation:** XML Schemas (XSD) can be used to define rules and constraints for XML documents, ensuring data integrity.
- **Legacy Systems:** XML is often used in legacy systems and enterprise applications, making it relevant for integrating IoT with existing infrastructure.

Choosing Between JSON and XML

The choice between JSON and XML depends on the specific requirements of your IoT application.

- **JSON is generally preferred for its simplicity, readability, and efficiency, especially in web-based IoT applications.**
- **XML might be more suitable when you need extensibility, data validation, or integration with legacy systems.**

In many cases, the choice may be dictated by the APIs and services you are interacting with. It's important to understand the strengths and limitations of both formats to make informed decisions in your IoT development.

Data Serialization and Deserialization

In the interconnected world of IoT, data is the lifeblood that fuels insights, automation, and decision-making. This data, generated by myriad sensors and devices, needs to be structured and organized in a way that facilitates efficient exchange and processing. This chapter explores two prominent data formats that play a crucial role in IoT data representation: JSON and XML. We'll delve into their structures, strengths, and how they are used to represent information within IoT systems.

JSON (JavaScript Object Notation)

JSON has emerged as a dominant data format in web development and IoT, favored for its simplicity, readability, and compatibility with JavaScript. It's a lightweight text-based format that represents data as key-value pairs, arrays, and nested objects, making it ideal for representing structured information.

Structure of JSON:

- **Key-Value Pairs:** Data is represented as key-value pairs, where the key is a string enclosed in double quotes, and the value can be a string, number, boolean, array, object, or null.

JSON

```
{
  "deviceId": "device123",
  "temperature": 25.5
}
```

- **Arrays:** Ordered lists of values enclosed in square brackets.

JSON

```
{
  "sensorReadings": [25.5, 26.2, 25.8]
}
```

- **Nested Objects:** Objects can be nested within other objects to represent hierarchical data structures.

JSON

```
{
  "device": {
    "id": "device123",
    "location": "living room",
    "sensors": {
      "temperature": 25.5,
      "humidity": 60
    }
  }
}
```

Strengths of JSON in IoT:

- **Lightweight:** JSON's concise syntax reduces data size, making it efficient for transmission over networks, especially in bandwidth-constrained IoT environments.
- **Readability:** JSON's simple structure is easy for both humans and machines to read and understand, facilitating debugging and data analysis.
- **JavaScript Compatibility:** JSON is natively supported by JavaScript, making it easy to parse and manipulate in web applications and Node.js environments.
- **Wide Adoption:** JSON is widely used in web APIs and data exchange, making it a versatile choice for IoT integration.

XML (Extensible Markup Language)

XML is a markup language that defines a set of rules for encoding documents in a format that is both human-readable and machine-readable. It uses tags to define elements and attributes to provide additional information about those elements.[1]

Structure of XML:

- **Elements:** Defined by start and end tags, e.g., `<temperature>25.5</temperature>`.
- **Attributes:** Provide additional information about elements, e.g., `<sensor id="sensor123">`.
- **Nested Elements:** Elements can be nested within other elements to create hierarchical structures.

XML

```
<device id="device123">
  <location>living room</location>
  <sensors>
    <temperature>25.5</temperature>
    <humidity>60</humidity>
  </sensors>
</device>
```

Strengths of XML in IoT:

- **Extensibility:** XML allows you to define your own tags and structures, making it adaptable to various data representation needs.
- **Data Validation:** XML Schemas (XSD) can be used to define rules and constraints for XML documents, ensuring data integrity.

- **Legacy Systems:** XML is often used in legacy systems and enterprise applications, making it relevant for integrating IoT with existing infrastructure.

Choosing Between JSON and XML

The choice between JSON and XML depends on the specific requirements of your IoT application.

- **JSON is generally preferred for its simplicity, readability, and efficiency, especially in web-based IoT applications.**
- **XML might be more suitable when you need extensibility, data validation, or integration with legacy systems.**

In many cases, the choice may be dictated by the APIs and services you are interacting with. It's important to understand the strengths and limitations of both formats to make informed decisions in your IoT development.

Storing and Managing IoT Data

The sheer volume and velocity of data generated by IoT devices necessitate robust strategies for storage and management. This section explores the various approaches to storing and managing

IoT data, considering factors like data volume, velocity, variety, and the specific needs of your IoT applications.

Data Storage Options

IoT data can be stored in various locations, each with its own trade-offs:

- **On-Device Storage:** Data is stored directly on the IoT device itself, typically using flash memory or embedded storage. This is suitable for applications with limited connectivity or where real-time access to recent data is crucial. However, on-device storage is limited by the device's storage capacity.
- **Edge Storage:** Data is stored on a gateway or edge device located close to the IoT devices. This reduces latency and bandwidth consumption compared to cloud storage. Edge storage is suitable for applications requiring real-time processing and decision-making at the edge.
- **Cloud Storage:** Data is stored in the cloud, offering scalability, accessibility, and powerful data management capabilities. Cloud storage providers like AWS, Azure, and Google Cloud offer various storage

solutions, including databases, data lakes, and object storage. This is ideal for applications requiring long-term storage, large-scale data analysis, and integration with other cloud services.

Data Management Considerations

Effective IoT data management involves several key considerations:

- **Data Volume:** IoT devices generate massive amounts of data. Choose storage solutions that can scale to accommodate this volume.
- **Data Velocity:** Data arrives at high speeds. Implement efficient data ingestion pipelines and real-time processing capabilities.
- **Data Variety:** IoT data comes in various formats (e.g., sensor readings, images, video). Choose storage and processing solutions that can handle this variety.
- **Data Security:** Protect your IoT data from unauthorized access and breaches. Implement security measures like encryption, access control, and authentication.

- **Data Retention:** Determine how long you need to store the data. Implement data retention policies and archiving strategies.
- **Data Governance:** Establish policies and procedures for data quality, access control, and compliance with regulations.

Data Management Technologies

Various technologies facilitate efficient IoT data management:

- **Databases:**
    - **Relational Databases (SQL):** Suitable for structured data with well-defined relationships. Examples: MySQL, PostgreSQL, Microsoft SQL Server.
    - **NoSQL Databases:** Offer flexibility and scalability for handling unstructured and semi-structured data. Examples: MongoDB, Cassandra, Couchbase.
    - **Time-Series Databases:** Optimized for storing and analyzing time-stamped data, common in IoT applications. Examples: InfluxDB, TimescaleDB.

- **Data Lakes:** Centralized repositories that store raw data in various formats, allowing for flexible data analysis and exploration.
- **Message Queues:** Facilitate asynchronous communication and data flow between IoT devices and applications. Examples: Kafka, RabbitMQ.
- **Data Processing Frameworks:** Enable distributed data processing and analysis. Examples: Apache Spark, Apache Flink.

Choosing the Right Approach

The optimal approach to storing and managing IoT data depends on the specific needs of your application. Consider factors like:

- **Data Volume and Velocity**
- **Data Structure and Variety**
- **Real-time Processing Requirements**
- **Storage Costs**
- **Security and Compliance Needs**

By carefully evaluating these factors and selecting the appropriate technologies, you can build a robust and scalable data management system for your IoT solutions.

Chapter VII. Building Real-World IoT Projects

Project 1: Home Automation System with Python and Raspberry Pi

This chapter marks the exciting transition from foundational concepts to hands-on applications. We'll embark on our first real-world IoT project: building a home automation system using Python and a Raspberry Pi. This project will solidify your understanding of Python programming for IoT, introduce you to working with sensors and actuators, and demonstrate how to integrate these components into a functional system.

Project 1: Home Automation System

Imagine controlling your home's lighting, temperature, and security systems with a few taps on your smartphone or through voice commands. This project will guide you through building a basic home automation system that you can customize and expand upon.

Project Goals:

- **Control a relay module to switch lights or appliances on and off.**
- **Read temperature and humidity data from a DHT11/DHT22 sensor.**
- **Display sensor readings and control the relay through a web interface.**

Hardware Requirements:

- Raspberry Pi (Model 3 or 4 recommended)
- DHT11 or DHT22 temperature and humidity sensor
- Relay module (e.g., 4-channel relay)
- Jumper wires
- LEDs (optional, for visual feedback)

Software Requirements:

- Raspberry Pi OS (with desktop environment recommended)
- Python 3
- `RPi.GPIO` library
- `Adafruit_DHT` library (or equivalent for your sensor)
- Flask (a Python web framework)

Step-by-Step Implementation

1. **Set up the Raspberry Pi:**

- Install Raspberry Pi OS on your Raspberry Pi.
- Connect to your Wi-Fi network.
- Update the system packages: `sudo apt update && sudo apt upgrade -y`
- Install Python 3 and pip: `sudo apt install python3 python3-pip -y`

2. **Connect the Hardware:**
   - Connect the DHT11/DHT22 sensor to the Raspberry Pi's GPIO pins according to the sensor's documentation.
   - Connect the relay module to the GPIO pins and the device you want to control (e.g., a lamp).
   - (Optional) Connect LEDs to the relay module for visual feedback.

3. **Install Python Libraries:**
   - Install the `RPi.GPIO` and `Adafruit_DHT` libraries:

Bash

```
pip3 install RPi.GPIO Adafruit_DHT
```

○

4. **Write the Python Code:**
   - ○ Create a Python script (e.g., `home_automation.py`) to:
     - ■ Initialize the GPIO pins and the sensor.
     - ■ Read temperature and humidity data from the sensor.
     - ■ Create a Flask web server with routes to:
       - ■ Display sensor readings on a web page.
       - ■ Control the relay module (turn devices on/off) through buttons or links on the web page.

Example Code Snippet (Flask web server):

Python

```python
from flask import Flask, render_template,
request
import RPi.GPIO as GPIO
import Adafruit_DHT
import time

app = Flask(__name__)
```

```python
# GPIO pin configuration
relay_pin = 17
GPIO.setmode(GPIO.BCM)
GPIO.setup(relay_pin, GPIO.OUT)

# DHT sensor configuration
sensor = Adafruit_DHT.DHT11
dht_pin = 4

# Initial state of the relay (off)
relay_state = False
GPIO.output(relay_pin, GPIO.LOW)

@app.route('/')
def index():
    # Read sensor data
    humidity, temperature = Adafruit_DHT.read_retry(sensor, dht_pin)

    # Render the web page with sensor data
and relay state
    return render_template('index.html',
temperature=temperature, humidity=humidity,
relay_state=relay_state)

@app.route('/control', methods=['POST'])
def control():
    global relay_state
    action = request.form['action']
    if action == 'on':
        GPIO.output(relay_pin, GPIO.HIGH)
        relay_state = True
    elif action == 'off':
```

```
        GPIO.output(relay_pin, GPIO.LOW)
        relay_state = False
    return index()

if __name__ == '__main__':
    app.run(debug=True, host='0.0.0.0')
```

5. **Create the Web Interface (index.html):**
   - Create an HTML file (e.g., `templates/index.html`) to display the sensor readings and provide buttons to control the relay.

Example Code Snippet (index.html):

HTML

```
<!DOCTYPE html>
<html>
<head>
    <title>Home Automation</title>
</head>
<body>
    <h1>Home Automation</h1>
    <p>Temperature: {{ temperature }}°C</p>
    <p>Humidity: {{ humidity }}%</p>

    <h2>Device Control</h2>
    <form method="POST" action="/control">
        {% if relay_state %}
```

```
                        <button type="submit"
name="action" value="off">Turn Off</button>
        {% else %}
                        <button type="submit"
name="action" value="on">Turn On</button>
        {% endif %}
    </form>
</body>
</html>
```

6. **Run the Application:**
   - Run the Python script: `python3 home_automation.py`
   - Access the web interface by opening a web browser and navigating to the Raspberry Pi's IP address (e.g., `http://192.168.1.100`).

This project provides a basic framework for a home automation system. You can expand upon it by adding more sensors, actuators, and features like:

- **Motion sensors for security.**
- **Light sensors for automatic lighting control.**
- **Integration with voice assistants like Amazon Alexa or Google Assistant.**
- **Remote access through the internet.**

This project serves as a practical starting point for exploring the possibilities of home automation with Python and Raspberry Pi. By combining your creativity with the knowledge gained from this book, you can build a truly smart and personalized home environment.

Project 2: Environmental Monitoring with ESP32 and JavaScript

Building upon our home automation project, we'll now explore a different application of IoT: environmental monitoring. This project utilizes an ESP32 microcontroller and JavaScript to create a system that collects temperature and humidity data and displays it on a dynamic web interface.

Project 2: Environmental Monitoring System

Environmental monitoring is crucial in various scenarios, from agriculture and smart homes to industrial settings and scientific research. This project will guide you through building a system that continuously monitors temperature and humidity, providing valuable insights into your environment.

Project Goals:

- Collect temperature and humidity data using a DHT11/DHT22 sensor connected to an ESP32.
- Send the sensor data to a web server using HTTP requests.
- Display the data on a web page with dynamic charts using JavaScript and Chart.js.

Hardware Requirements:

- ESP32 development board
- DHT11 or DHT22 temperature and humidity sensor
- Breadboard and jumper wires
- (Optional) 3.3V power supply (if not powering via USB)

Software Requirements:

- Arduino IDE
- ESP32 board support in Arduino IDE
- Node.js and npm (Node Package Manager)
- Express.js (web framework for Node.js)
- Chart.js (JavaScript library for charts)

Step-by-Step Implementation

1. **Set up the ESP32:**

- Install the ESP32 board support in your Arduino IDE.
- Connect the DHT11/DHT22 sensor to the ESP32's pins according to the sensor's documentation.
- Write the Arduino code to:
  - Initialize the Wi-Fi connection.
  - Read data from the DHT sensor.
  - Send the sensor data to a web server using HTTP POST requests (we'll set up the server in the next step).

Example Code Snippet (Arduino):

C++

```cpp
#include <WiFi.h>
#include <HTTPClient.h>
#include "DHT.h"

#define DHTPIN 4 // Digital pin connected
to the DHT sensor
#define DHTTYPE1 DHT11   // DHT 11

const char* ssid = "YOUR_WIFI_SSID";
const      char*      password      =
"YOUR_WIFI_PASSWORD";
```

```cpp
const        char*        serverName       =
"http://your-server-ip-address:3000/data";
// Replace with your server address

DHT dht(DHTPIN, DHTTYPE);
WiFiClient client;

void setup() {
  Serial.begin(115200);
  dht.begin();
  WiFi.begin(ssid, password);
  while (WiFi.status() != WL_CONNECTED) {
    delay(500);[2]
    Serial.print(".");
  }
  Serial.println("WiFi connected");
  Serial.println("IP address: ");
  Serial.println(WiFi.localIP());
}

void[3] loop() {
    // Wait a few seconds between
measurements.
  delay(2000);

  // Reading temperature or humidity takes
about 250 milliseconds!
  // Sensor readings may also be up to 2
seconds 'old' (its a very slow sensor)
  float h = dht.readHumidity();
    // Read temperature as Celsius (the
default)
  float t = dht.readTemperature();
```

```
  // Check if any reads failed and exit
early (to try again).
  if (isnan(h) || isnan(t)) {
    Serial.println(F("Failed[4] to read from
DHT sensor!"));
    return;
  }


  // Send[5] data to the server
  if(client.connect(serverName, 3000)) {
    String postData = "temperature=" +
String(t) + "&humidity=" + String(h);
    client.println("POST /data HTTP/1.1");
                    client.println("Host:
your-server-ip-address:3000");  // Replace
with your server address
            client.println("Content-Type:
application/x-www-form-urlencoded");
    client.println("Content-Length: " +
String(postData.length()));
    client.println();
    client.println(postData);
    Serial.println("Data[6] sent to server");
  } else {
    Serial.println("Connection to server
failed");
  }
  client.stop();
}
```

2. **Set up the Web Server:**
   ○ Create a Node.js project and install Express.js: `npm install express`
   ○ Create a JavaScript file (e.g., `server.js`) to:
     - Create an Express.js server.
     - Define a route to handle POST requests from the ESP32 (e.g., `/data`).
     - Store the received sensor data in an array or database.
     - Serve a web page (e.g., `index.html`) that will display the data.

Example Code Snippet (server.js):

JavaScript

```javascript
const express = require('express');
const app = express();
const port = 3000;

// Array to store sensor data
let sensorData = [];

app.use(express.urlencoded({ extended: true
}));

app.post('/data', (req, res) => {
```

```
                const        temperature        =
parseFloat(req.body.temperature);
                const         humidity         =
parseFloat(req.body.humidity);
    sensorData.push({ temperature, humidity,
timestamp: new Date() });
          console.log('Received        data:',
temperature, humidity);
    res.sendStatus(200);
});

app.get('/', (req, res) => {
    res.sendFile(__dirname + '/index.html');
});

app.listen(port, () => {
    console.log(`Server  listening  on  port
${port}`);
});
```

3. **Create the Web Interface (index.html):**
   ○ Create an HTML file (e.g., `index.html`) to display the sensor data.
   ○ Include Chart.js in your HTML file.
   ○ Use JavaScript to:
      ■ Fetch sensor data from the server.

- Create dynamic charts using Chart.js to visualize the temperature and humidity data.

Example Code Snippet (index.html with Chart.js):

HTML

```
<!DOCTYPE html>
<html>
<head>
  <title>Environmental Monitoring</title>
                              <script
src="https://cdn.jsdelivr.net/npm/chart.js"
></script>
</head>
<body>
  <h1>Environmental Monitoring</h1>
  <canvas id="myChart"></canvas>

  <script>
                      const    ctx    =
document.getElementById('myChart').getConte
xt('2d');
    const chart = new Chart(ctx, {
      type: 'line',
      data: {
        labels:7 [], // Time labels
        datasets: [{
          label: 'Temperature (°C)',
          data: [], // Temperature data
```

```
        borderColor: 'rgb(255, 99, 132)',
        fill: false
      }, {
        label: 'Humidity (%)',
        data: [], // Humidity data
        borderColor: 'rgb(54, 162, 235)',
        fill: false
      }]
    },
    options: {
      scales: {
        x: {
          type: 'time',
          time: {
            unit: 'minute'
          }
        }
      }
    }
  });

    // Fetch data from the server and
update the chart
    function updateChart() {
      fetch('/data')
        .then(response => response.json())
        .then(data => {
          chart.data.labels = data.map(item
=> item.timestamp);
            chart.data.datasets[0].data =
data.map(item => item.temperature);
            chart.data.datasets[1].data =
data.map(item => item.humidity);
```

```
      chart.update();
    });
  }

  // Update the chart every 5 seconds
  setInterval(updateChart, 5000);
</script>
</body>
</html>
```

4. **Run the Application:**
   - Upload the Arduino code to your ESP32.
   - Run the Node.js server: `node server.js`
   - Open a web browser and navigate to `http://localhost:3000` to view the environmental monitoring dashboard.

This project demonstrates how to combine the capabilities of an ESP32 microcontroller with JavaScript and web technologies to create a functional environmental monitoring system. You can further enhance this project by:

- Adding more sensors (e.g., light, pressure, air quality).

- Implementing data storage using a database.
- Adding user authentication and authorization.
- Creating a mobile-friendly interface.

By exploring these enhancements, you can gain a deeper understanding of IoT development and create more sophisticated and impactful solutions.

Project 3: Smart Agriculture System with Arduino and Cloud Integration

Our final project in this chapter ventures into the realm of smart agriculture, where technology intersects with traditional farming practices to enhance efficiency and productivity. This project combines the versatility of an Arduino microcontroller with the power of cloud integration to create a system that monitors soil moisture and automatically controls irrigation.

Project 3: Smart Agriculture System

Water is a precious resource, especially in agriculture. This project aims to optimize water usage by automatically irrigating crops based on real-time soil moisture readings. By integrating with a cloud platform, you can monitor your farm remotely and gain valuable insights into your crops' water needs.

Project Goals:

- **Measure soil moisture using a soil moisture sensor connected to an Arduino.**
- **Control a water pump based on soil moisture levels.**
- **Send sensor data and irrigation status to the cloud (ThingSpeak in this example).**
- **Visualize data and control irrigation remotely through a ThingSpeak dashboard.**

Hardware Requirements:

- Arduino Uno (or similar)
- Soil moisture sensor
- Water pump
- Relay module
- Jumper wires
- ESP8266 Wi-Fi module (or similar)

Software Requirements:

- Arduino IDE
- ThingSpeak account
- ThingSpeak library for Arduino

Step-by-Step Implementation

1. Set up the Arduino:

- Connect the soil moisture sensor, relay module, and water pump to the Arduino according to the wiring diagram.
- Connect the ESP8266 Wi-Fi module to the Arduino for internet connectivity.
- Write the Arduino code to:
  - Read soil moisture levels from the sensor.
  - Control the relay module to turn the water pump on/off based on predefined thresholds.
  - Send sensor data and pump status to ThingSpeak using the ThingSpeak library.

Example Code Snippet (Arduino):

C++

```cpp
#include <ESP8266WiFi.h>
#include <ThingSpeak.h>

// Replace with your network credentials
const char* ssid = "YOUR_WIFI_SSID";
```

```cpp
const      char*       password       =
"YOUR_WIFI_PASSWORD";

// ThingSpeak API keys
unsigned    long     myChannelNumber      =
YOUR_CHANNEL_NUMBER;
const     char    *     myWriteAPIKey      =
"YOUR_WRITE_API_KEY";

WiFiClient  client;

const int sensorPin = A0;  // Soil moisture
sensor connected to analog pin A0
const int pumpPin = 7;     // Relay module
connected to digital pin 7

void setup() {
  Serial.begin(9600);  // Initialize serial
communication

  // Connect to Wi-Fi
  WiFi.begin(ssid, password);
  while (WiFi.status() != WL_CONNECTED) {
    delay(500);
    Serial.print(".");
  }
  Serial.println("WiFi connected");

   ThingSpeak.begin(client);   // Initialize
ThingSpeak
}

void loop() {
```

```
  // Read soil moisture level
  int sensorValue = analogRead(sensorPin);
        float     moisturePercentage     =
map(sensorValue,   1023,   0,   0,   100);   //
Assuming higher value means drier soil

  // Control the water pump
  if (moisturePercentage < 30) { // If soil
is dry
    digitalWrite(pumpPin, HIGH); // Turn on
the pump
  } else {
      digitalWrite(pumpPin, LOW);   // Turn
off the pump
  }

  // Send data to ThingSpeak
  ThingSpeak.writeField(myChannelNumber, 1,
moisturePercentage, myWriteAPIKey);
  ThingSpeak.writeField(myChannelNumber, 2,
digitalRead(pumpPin), myWriteAPIKey);

  delay(20000); // Update every 20 seconds
}
```

2. **Set up ThingSpeak:**
   ○ Create a ThingSpeak account.
   ○ Create a new channel and define two
     fields: "Soil Moisture" and "Pump
     Status."

3. **Visualize Data and Control Irrigation:**
    - Use ThingSpeak's built-in visualizations to create charts and graphs of your sensor data.
    - Use ThingSpeak's React app to create a custom dashboard with additional features like:
        - Real-time data display.
        - Historical data analysis.
        - Manual pump control.
        - Alerts and notifications based on soil moisture levels.

Expanding the System

This project provides a foundation for a smart agriculture system. You can expand upon it by:

- **Adding more sensors:** Incorporate sensors for temperature, humidity, light intensity, and nutrient levels.
- **Implementing more sophisticated control algorithms:** Use machine learning to predict irrigation needs based on historical data and weather patterns.
- **Integrating with other cloud services:** Connect to weather APIs to incorporate weather data into your irrigation decisions.

- **Building a mobile app:** Create a mobile application for remote monitoring and control.

This project demonstrates the power of combining Arduino with cloud integration to create a practical and impactful IoT solution for smart agriculture. By leveraging the flexibility of Arduino and the scalability of the cloud, you can build sophisticated systems that optimize resource usage, improve crop yields, and contribute to sustainable farming practices.

Chapter VIII. IoT Security: Protecting Your Devices and Data

Common IoT Security Threats and Vulnerabilities

The proliferation of IoT devices has brought about a new era of connectivity and convenience, but it has also introduced a significant attack surface for malicious actors. This chapter delves into the critical realm of IoT security, exploring common threats and vulnerabilities that can compromise your devices, data, and overall system integrity. Understanding these threats is the first step towards building secure and resilient IoT solutions.

The Expanding Attack Surface

The interconnected nature of IoT devices creates an expansive attack surface that extends beyond traditional IT infrastructure. Each connected device, sensor, and communication channel represents a potential entry point for attackers. This complexity demands a comprehensive approach to security that addresses vulnerabilities at every layer of the IoT ecosystem.

Common IoT Security Threats and Vulnerabilities

1. **Weak Passwords and Authentication:** Many IoT devices come with default passwords or weak authentication mechanisms, making them easy targets for attackers. Brute-force attacks, dictionary attacks, and credential stuffing can be used to gain unauthorized access to devices.
2. **Insecure Network Services:** IoT devices often expose unnecessary network services or use insecure protocols, leaving them vulnerable to attacks like eavesdropping, man-in-the-middle attacks, and denial-of-service attacks.
3. **Outdated Firmware and Software:** Many IoT devices are deployed with outdated firmware or software that may contain known vulnerabilities. Attackers can exploit these vulnerabilities to gain control of devices or access sensitive data.
4. **Insecure Data Storage and Transmission:** Data stored on IoT devices or transmitted over networks may be vulnerable to unauthorized access or modification if not properly protected. Encryption, access control, and secure communication protocols are essential for safeguarding data.
5. **Lack of Device Management:** Insufficient device management capabilities can hinder

security monitoring, firmware updates, and vulnerability patching. This can leave devices exposed to attacks and compromise the overall system security.

6. **Insecure Ecosystem Interfaces:** The interfaces between IoT devices, applications, and cloud platforms can introduce vulnerabilities if not properly secured. This includes web interfaces, APIs, and mobile applications.

7. **Insufficient Privacy Protection:** IoT devices often collect sensitive personal data. Inadequate privacy protection measures can lead to data breaches and privacy violations.

8. **Physical Security:** Physical access to IoT devices can also pose a security risk. Tampering with devices, extracting firmware, or installing malicious hardware can compromise the entire system.

9. **Botnets and DDoS Attacks:** Compromised IoT devices can be recruited into botnets, which can then be used to launch distributed denial-of-service (DDoS) attacks against other systems or networks.

10. **Lack of Security Awareness:** Users and developers may not be aware of the security risks associated with IoT devices, leading to

poor security practices and configuration errors.

Examples of Attacks

- **Mirai Botnet:** A notorious botnet that exploited weak passwords in IoT devices to launch massive DDoS attacks.
- **BrickerBot:** Malware that permanently "bricked" (rendered unusable) vulnerable IoT devices.
- **VPNFilter:** Sophisticated malware that infected routers and other network devices, allowing attackers to steal data and launch attacks.

Addressing IoT Security Challenges

Addressing these threats requires a multi-faceted approach that includes:

- **Strong Passwords and Authentication:** Use strong, unique passwords and implement multi-factor authentication.
- **Secure Communication Protocols:** Use secure protocols like HTTPS and TLS/SSL for data transmission.

- **Regular Firmware Updates:** Keep device firmware and software up to date to patch vulnerabilities.
- **Data Encryption:** Encrypt data at rest and in transit to protect it from unauthorized access.
- **Device Management:** Implement robust device management capabilities for monitoring, updates, and security management.
- **Security Awareness Training:** Educate users and developers about IoT security best practices.

By understanding the common threats and vulnerabilities in IoT and implementing appropriate security measures, you can significantly reduce the risk of attacks and protect your devices, data, and overall system integrity.

Implementing Secure Communication Protocols (TLS/SSL)

In the previous section, we explored the diverse landscape of IoT security threats. Now, we shift our focus to implementing one of the most crucial security measures: secure communication protocols. This section delves into TLS/SSL (Transport Layer Security/Secure Sockets Layer), a cryptographic protocol that forms the bedrock of secure communication over the internet, and its pivotal role in safeguarding IoT data.

TLS/SSL: The Guardian of Online Communication

TLS/SSL is a protocol that provides a secure channel for communication between two parties over a network. It's widely used to protect sensitive data like credit card information, login credentials, and personal information during online transactions and interactions. In the context of IoT, TLS/SSL plays a vital role in securing communication between devices, applications, and the cloud.

How TLS/SSL Works:

1. **Handshake:** The client and server initiate a "handshake" process to establish a secure connection. During this process, they:
   - Negotiate the TLS/SSL version to use.
   - Select a cipher suite for encryption.
   - Authenticate each other using digital certificates.
   - Exchange cryptographic keys for encrypting and decrypting data.
2. **Encryption:** Once the secure connection is established, all data exchanged between the

client and server is encrypted using the negotiated cipher suite. This ensures that even if the data is intercepted, it cannot be read or tampered with by unauthorized parties.
3. **Data Integrity:** TLS/SSL also incorporates mechanisms to ensure data integrity. This means that any changes to the data during transmission will be detected, preventing data corruption or manipulation.

Benefits of TLS/SSL in IoT

- **Confidentiality:** Encryption ensures that only authorized parties can read the data being transmitted.
- **Integrity:** Data integrity mechanisms prevent data tampering and ensure that the received data is the same as the sent data.
- **Authentication:** Digital certificates authenticate the identities of the communicating parties, preventing impersonation and man-in-the-middle attacks.
- **Trust:** TLS/SSL establishes a trusted connection, giving users confidence that their data is secure.

Implementing TLS/SSL in IoT

Implementing TLS/SSL in your IoT solutions involves several steps:

1. **Obtain SSL Certificates:** Obtain SSL certificates from a trusted Certificate Authority (CA). These certificates are digital documents that verify the identity of your devices or servers.
2. **Configure Devices and Servers:** Configure your IoT devices and servers to use TLS/SSL. This typically involves enabling TLS/SSL support in the device's firmware or server's configuration.
3. **Use Secure Libraries and APIs:** Utilize libraries and APIs that support TLS/SSL for communication. For example, use the `ssl` module in Python or secure HTTP libraries in other languages.
4. **Secure Web Interfaces:** If your IoT solution includes web interfaces, ensure they are served over HTTPS (HTTP Secure), which uses TLS/SSL to encrypt communication between the browser and the server.
5. **Secure MQTT Communication:** If you are using MQTT, consider using MQTT over TLS/SSL to secure the communication between devices and the MQTT broker.

Example: Securing an HTTP Connection with Python

Python

```python
import requests

# Replace with your server address
url = 'https://your-iot-server.com/data'

# Send an HTTPS request
response = requests.get(url, verify=True)

# Verify the server's certificate
if response.status_code == 200:
    print("Secure connection established!")
else:
    print("Error: Could not establish a
secure connection.")
```

This code snippet demonstrates how to use the `requests` library in Python to send an HTTPS request. The `verify=True` parameter ensures that the server's SSL certificate is verified.

By implementing TLS/SSL in your IoT solutions, you add a critical layer of security that protects your data from unauthorized access, tampering, and eavesdropping. This ensures the confidentiality, integrity, and authenticity of your IoT communication, building trust and resilience in your connected systems.

Data Encryption and Authentication Techniques

Building upon our exploration of secure communication protocols, we now delve deeper into the critical components of data protection: encryption and authentication techniques. These techniques are essential for safeguarding sensitive information in IoT systems, ensuring confidentiality, integrity, and trust.

Data Encryption: Shielding Information from Prying Eyes

Data encryption is the process of converting plaintext data into an unreadable format called ciphertext. This transformation is achieved using cryptographic algorithms and keys. Only authorized parties with the corresponding decryption key can convert the ciphertext back into its original plaintext form.

Types of Encryption:

- **Symmetric Encryption:** Uses the same key for both encryption and decryption. This method is efficient for encrypting large amounts of data but requires secure key distribution. Examples: AES, DES.
- **Asymmetric Encryption:** Uses a pair of keys: a public key for encryption and a private key for decryption. The public key can be widely distributed, while the private key is kept secret. This method is suitable for secure key exchange and digital signatures. Examples: RSA, ECC.

Encryption in IoT:

- **Data at Rest:** Encrypting data stored on devices or in the cloud protects it from unauthorized access even if the device or storage is compromised.
- **Data in Transit:** Encrypting data transmitted over networks prevents eavesdropping and man-in-the-middle attacks.

Authentication: Verifying Identities

Authentication is the process of verifying the identity of a user, device, or system. It ensures that only authorized entities can access resources or perform actions.

Authentication Techniques:

- **Passwords:** A common authentication method, but passwords should be strong, unique, and regularly updated.
- **Multi-factor Authentication (MFA):** Requires multiple factors for authentication, such as something you know (password), something you have (security token), or something you are (biometric).
- **Digital Certificates:** Electronic documents that verify the identity of a device or server. Used in TLS/SSL to authenticate communicating parties.
- **API Keys:** Unique identifiers used to authenticate applications or services accessing an API.
- **Biometrics:** Uses unique biological traits (e.g., fingerprint, facial recognition) for authentication.

Authentication in IoT:

- **Device Authentication:** Verify the identity of devices connecting to the network or cloud platform.
- **User Authentication:** Authenticate users accessing IoT devices or applications.

- **API Authentication:** Authenticate applications or services accessing IoT data or functionalities.

Combining Encryption and Authentication

Encryption and authentication are often used together to provide comprehensive data protection. For example, TLS/SSL uses both encryption and digital certificates to secure communication.

Example: Encrypting Data with AES in Python

Python

```python
from cryptography.fernet import Fernet

# Generate a key
key = Fernet.generate_key()

# Create a Fernet object
cipher_suite = Fernet(key)

# Encrypt the data
message = "This is a secret message".encode()
encrypted_message = cipher_suite.encrypt(message)

# Decrypt the data
decrypted_message = cipher_suite.decrypt(encrypted_message)
```

```
print("Original                    message:",
message.decode())
print("Encrypted                   message:",
encrypted_message)
print("Decrypted                   message:",
decrypted_message.decode())
```

This code snippet demonstrates how to use the `cryptography` library in Python to encrypt and decrypt data using the AES algorithm.

By implementing robust encryption and authentication techniques, you can build secure IoT solutions that protect sensitive data, prevent unauthorized access, and maintain the integrity of your connected systems. These measures are essential for building trust and ensuring the responsible deployment of IoT technologies.

Chapter IX. Data Analytics and Visualization for IoT

The true power of the Internet of Things lies not just in connecting devices but in extracting meaningful insights from the vast amounts of data they generate. This chapter delves into the crucial process of collecting and processing IoT data, laying the foundation for analysis and visualization that can drive informed decision-making and optimize IoT systems.

Collecting IoT Data: The First Step to Insight

Collecting data from your IoT devices is the initial step in the data analytics pipeline. This process involves gathering raw data from various sources, such as sensors, actuators, and other connected devices. The method of collection depends on the type of device, network connectivity, and the nature of the data itself.

Common Data Collection Methods:

- **Direct Connection:** Devices can be directly connected to a computer or server for data retrieval, often using protocols like USB or serial communication.

- **Network Protocols:** Devices can transmit data over various network protocols, including:
  - **MQTT:** Lightweight protocol for efficient data transfer in resource-constrained environments.
  - **HTTP:** Versatile protocol for sending data to web servers or cloud platforms.
  - **CoAP:** Specialized protocol for constrained devices and networks.
- **Cloud Platforms:** Cloud providers like AWS, Azure, and Google Cloud offer services for collecting and ingesting data from IoT devices.

Considerations for Data Collection:

- **Data Frequency:** Determine how often you need to collect data. This depends on the nature of the data and the application's requirements.
- **Data Format:** Choose a suitable data format for efficient storage and processing (e.g., JSON, CSV).

- **Data Security:** Implement security measures to protect data during transmission and storage (e.g., encryption, authentication).
- **Data Volume:** Estimate the volume of data you'll be collecting to choose appropriate storage and processing solutions.

Processing IoT Data: Transforming Raw Data into Information

Once collected, raw IoT data often requires processing to make it usable for analysis and visualization. This processing can involve various steps, depending on the nature of the data and the desired outcome.

Common Data Processing Steps:

- **Data Cleaning:** Remove errors, inconsistencies, and irrelevant information from the data.
- **Data Transformation:** Convert data into a suitable format for analysis (e.g., convert units, aggregate data).
- **Data Reduction:** Reduce the size of the dataset by selecting relevant features or aggregating data.

- **Data Normalization:** Scale data to a common range to improve analysis and model performance.
- **Data Aggregation:** Combine data from multiple sources or time periods to gain a broader perspective.

Tools for Data Processing:

- **Programming Languages:** Python, with libraries like Pandas and NumPy, is widely used for data processing.
- **Cloud Platforms:** Cloud providers offer data processing services like AWS Lambda, Azure Functions, and Google Cloud Functions.
- **Data Processing Frameworks:** Apache Spark and Apache Flink provide distributed data processing capabilities for large-scale datasets.

Example: Processing Temperature Data

Imagine you have collected temperature data from multiple sensors in a building. The processing steps might include:

1. **Data Cleaning:** Remove any erroneous readings or outliers.

2. **Data Aggregation:** Calculate the average temperature for each room or floor.
3. **Data Transformation:** Convert temperatures from Celsius to Fahrenheit if needed.
4. **Data Normalization:** Scale the temperature values to a common range for comparison across different sensors.

This processed data is now ready for analysis and visualization, enabling you to identify trends, anomalies, and insights that can inform decisions about building management and energy efficiency.

By mastering the techniques of collecting and processing IoT data, you lay the groundwork for extracting valuable insights and optimizing your IoT systems. This processed data becomes the foundation for analysis and visualization, enabling you to unlock the full potential of your connected devices.

Visualizing IoT Data with Charts and Graphs

Having collected and processed your IoT data, the next crucial step is to visualize it. Visualizations transform raw data into insightful representations, making it easier to identify patterns, trends, and anomalies. This section explores various techniques for visualizing IoT data with charts and graphs, empowering you to unlock the stories hidden within your data.

The Power of Visual Representation

Visualizing data offers several advantages:

- **Improved Understanding:** Charts and graphs make complex data more accessible and easier to comprehend.
- **Pattern Identification:** Visualizations help identify patterns, trends, and correlations that might not be apparent in raw data.
- **Faster Insights:** Visual representations allow for quicker data analysis and decision-making.
- **Effective Communication:** Charts and graphs are powerful tools for communicating data-driven insights to stakeholders.

Choosing the Right Chart

The choice of chart depends on the type of data you want to visualize and the insights you want to extract. Here are some common chart types used in IoT data visualization:

- **Line Charts:** Ideal for visualizing trends and changes over time. Often used to display time-series data like temperature readings, energy consumption, or sensor values over a period.
- **Bar Charts:** Effective for comparing different categories or groups of data. Useful for visualizing data like the number of devices connected to a network, the average sensor readings across different locations, or the distribution of data values.
- **Pie Charts:** Suitable for showing proportions and percentages. Can be used to visualize data like the distribution of device types, the percentage of devices online, or the breakdown of energy consumption by different appliances.
- **Scatter Plots:** Useful for identifying correlations between two variables. Can be used to visualize the relationship between temperature and humidity, or the correlation between sensor readings and device performance.
- **Heatmaps:** Effective for visualizing data density or distribution across a geographical area or a matrix. Can be used to display sensor readings across a field, the

distribution of devices in a building, or the correlation between different sensor values.

- **Gauges:** Suitable for displaying single values within a predefined range. Often used to visualize real-time data like temperature, pressure, or battery level.

Tools for Data Visualization

Several tools and libraries are available for creating visualizations from IoT data:

- **Programming Languages:** Python, with libraries like Matplotlib and Seaborn, is widely used for creating charts and graphs.
- **JavaScript Libraries:** Chart.js, D3.js, and Plotly.js are popular JavaScript libraries for creating interactive and dynamic visualizations in web applications.
- **Cloud Platforms:** Cloud providers offer data visualization tools and dashboards within their IoT platforms.
- **Data Visualization Tools:** Tableau, Power BI, and Qlik Sense are dedicated data visualization tools that can connect to various data sources, including IoT platforms.

Example: Visualizing Temperature and Humidity Data

Imagine you have collected temperature and humidity data from an environmental monitoring system. You could use a line chart to visualize the trends of both variables over time, a scatter plot to identify any correlation between them, and a gauge to display the current temperature and humidity readings.

By mastering the art of visualizing IoT data with charts and graphs, you can transform raw data into actionable insights, communicate findings effectively, and make informed decisions based on a clear understanding of your IoT systems.

Basic Data Analysis Techniques for IoT

Visualizing your IoT data provides a powerful way to understand it, but to truly unlock its potential, we need to go further with data analysis. This section explores some fundamental data analysis techniques that can help you extract meaningful insights from your IoT data, enabling you to identify trends, detect anomalies, and make data-driven decisions.

Descriptive Statistics: Summarizing Your Data

Descriptive statistics provide a concise summary of your data, helping you understand its central tendencies, dispersion, and distribution. Some common descriptive statistics include:

- **Mean:** The average value of a dataset.
- **Median:** The middle value in a sorted dataset.
- **Mode:** The most frequent value in a dataset.
- **Standard Deviation:** A measure of how spread out the data is from the mean.
- **Percentiles:** Values that divide a dataset into 100 equal parts.

Example: Analyzing Temperature Data

Imagine you have collected temperature data from a sensor over a week. Calculating the mean, median, and standard deviation can give you a quick overview of the average temperature, the typical temperature range, and how much the temperature fluctuates.

Using SQL Server Management Studio (SSMS):

SQL

```
-- Assuming your data is in a table called
'TemperatureReadings'   with   a   column
'Temperature'
```

```
SELECT
    AVG(Temperature) AS AverageTemperature,
        PERCENTILE_CONT(0.5)  WITHIN  GROUP
(ORDER        BY        Temperature)        AS
MedianTemperature,
    STDEV(Temperature) AS StandardDeviation
FROM TemperatureReadings;
```

This query calculates the average, median, and standard deviation of the `Temperature` column in the `TemperatureReadings` table.

Time Series Analysis: Unveiling Trends and Patterns

Time series analysis focuses on analyzing data collected over time to identify trends, seasonality, and other patterns. This is particularly relevant for IoT data, which is often time-stamped.

Techniques:

- **Moving Averages:** Calculate the average of data points over a specific time window to smooth out fluctuations and highlight trends.

- **Trend Lines:** Fit lines to the data to visualize the overall trend (increasing, decreasing, or stable).
- **Seasonality Analysis:** Identify recurring patterns in the data that occur at regular intervals (e.g., daily, weekly, or yearly).

Example: Analyzing Energy Consumption

Analyzing energy consumption data over time can reveal daily or weekly patterns, identify periods of high usage, and detect anomalies that might indicate equipment malfunctions or inefficiencies.

Correlation Analysis: Exploring Relationships

Correlation analysis examines the relationship between two or more variables. It helps you understand how changes in one variable are related to changes in another.

Correlation Coefficient: A statistical measure that indicates the strength and direction of the relationship between variables. Values range from -1 (perfect negative correlation) to 1 (perfect positive correlation), with 0 indicating no correlation.

Example: Analyzing Temperature and Humidity

Analyzing the correlation between temperature and humidity readings from an environmental monitoring system can reveal how these two variables influence each other.

Using SSMS:

SQL

```
-- Assuming your data is in a table called
'EnvironmentalData'          with          columns
'Temperature' and 'Humidity'
SELECT
         CORR(Temperature,  Humidity)  AS
CorrelationCoefficient
FROM EnvironmentalData;
```

This query calculates the correlation coefficient between the Temperature and Humidity columns in the EnvironmentalData table.

Anomaly Detection: Identifying the Unusual

Anomaly detection involves identifying data points that deviate significantly from the norm or expected patterns. This can be crucial for detecting equipment failures, security breaches, or other unusual events.

Techniques:

- **Thresholding:** Set thresholds for specific variables and flag data points that exceed those thresholds.
- **Clustering:** Group similar data points together and identify outliers that don't belong to any cluster.
- **Machine Learning:** Train machine learning models to identify anomalies based on historical data.

Example: Detecting Equipment Malfunctions

Analyzing sensor data from industrial equipment can help detect anomalies that might indicate a malfunction, allowing for proactive maintenance and preventing costly downtime.

By applying these basic data analysis techniques to your IoT data, you can extract valuable insights, optimize your systems, and make data-driven decisions.

Chapter X. Edge Computing in IoT

As the Internet of Things expands, generating massive amounts of data, a new paradigm is emerging to address the challenges of latency, bandwidth, and real-time processing: edge computing. This chapter introduces the core concepts of edge computing, exploring its significance in the IoT landscape and how it complements traditional cloud computing.

From Cloud to Edge: A Paradigm Shift

Traditional cloud computing relies on centralized data centers to process and store data. While this model offers scalability and powerful resources, it can introduce latency, especially for time-sensitive IoT applications. Edge computing addresses this by bringing computation closer to the data source – the "edge" of the network.

What is Edge Computing?

Edge computing involves processing data at or near the source of data generation, such as on IoT devices, gateways, or edge servers located closer to the devices. This decentralized approach reduces the distance data needs to travel, minimizing latency and enabling real-time processing.

Key Characteristics of Edge Computing:

- **Decentralized Processing:** Data is processed locally, reducing reliance on the cloud for every task.
- **Reduced Latency:** Processing data closer to the source minimizes delays, enabling real-time applications.
- **Bandwidth Optimization:** Less data needs to be transmitted to the cloud, conserving bandwidth and reducing costs.
- **Increased Autonomy:** Edge devices can operate independently, even with intermittent connectivity.
- **Enhanced Security:** Sensitive data can be processed locally, reducing the risk of data breaches during transmission.

The Edge Computing Continuum

Edge computing is not a single point but rather a continuum that spans from the device itself to the cloud. Different levels of the edge offer varying processing capabilities and resources:

- **Device Edge:** Computation occurs directly on the IoT device, leveraging its onboard processing power.
- **Gateway Edge:** Data is processed on a gateway device that aggregates data from multiple sensors or devices.
- **Network Edge:** Processing occurs on servers located at the edge of the network, closer to the devices than centralized cloud data centers.

Why Edge Computing Matters for IoT

Edge computing offers several benefits for IoT applications:

- **Real-time Responsiveness:** Critical for applications requiring immediate action, such as industrial automation, autonomous vehicles, and healthcare monitoring.
- **Bandwidth Efficiency:** Reduces the amount of data transmitted to the cloud, especially important for applications generating large volumes of data, such as video surveillance and environmental monitoring.
- **Offline Functionality:** Enables devices to function even when disconnected from the

cloud, crucial for remote or mobile deployments.

- **Enhanced Security:** Sensitive data can be processed locally, reducing the risk of data breaches during transmission.
- **Cost Savings:** Reduces data transmission costs and cloud processing expenses.

Edge Computing Use Cases

- **Industrial Automation:** Real-time control of machinery and processes, predictive maintenance, and anomaly detection.
- **Autonomous Vehicles:** Real-time processing of sensor data for navigation and decision-making.
- **Smart Cities:** Traffic management, environmental monitoring, and public safety applications.
- **Healthcare:** Remote patient monitoring, real-time health data analysis, and emergency response systems.
- **Retail Analytics:** In-store analytics, personalized customer experiences, and inventory management.

By understanding the core concepts of edge computing, you can leverage its capabilities to build more efficient, responsive, and secure IoT solutions. In the following sections, we'll explore how to implement edge computing using Python and JavaScript, and delve into the benefits and challenges of this paradigm.

Implementing Edge Computing with Python and JavaScript

Now that we've established the foundational concepts of edge computing, let's explore how to put these concepts into practice using Python and JavaScript. This section demonstrates how these versatile languages can be employed to implement edge computing functionalities in your IoT solutions.

Python: Powering Edge Intelligence

Python, with its extensive libraries and frameworks, is well-suited for implementing edge computing logic. Its versatility allows you to perform tasks such as data processing, analysis, and machine learning directly on edge devices.

Key Python Tools for Edge Computing:

- **MicroPython:** A lean and efficient implementation of Python 3 designed to run on microcontrollers and in constrained environments. This makes it ideal for deploying Python code directly on edge devices.

- **Libraries for Hardware Interaction:** Libraries like `RPi.GPIO` and `smbus2` enable interaction with sensors and actuators on edge devices, allowing for local data acquisition and control.
- **Data Processing and Analysis Libraries:** NumPy and Pandas provide powerful tools for manipulating and analyzing data at the edge.
- **Machine Learning Libraries:** Scikit-learn and TensorFlow Lite enable the deployment of machine learning models on edge devices for tasks like image recognition, anomaly detection, and predictive maintenance.

Example: Edge-Based Anomaly Detection with Python

Imagine you have an industrial sensor monitoring equipment vibrations. You can deploy a machine learning model using TensorFlow Lite on a Raspberry Pi to analyze the sensor data in real-time. If the model detects anomalous vibrations, it can trigger an alert or take corrective action locally, without needing to send all the data to the cloud.

162

JavaScript: Extending Edge Capabilities

JavaScript, particularly with Node.js, plays a crucial role in edge computing by enabling server-side functionalities and facilitating communication between edge devices and other systems.

Key JavaScript Tools for Edge Computing:

- **Node.js:** Allows you to run JavaScript on edge devices, enabling server-side logic and communication protocols.
- **Express.js:** A popular web framework for Node.js that can be used to create APIs and web applications on edge devices.
- **Socket.IO:** Enables real-time, bidirectional communication between edge devices and other systems, such as web applications or cloud platforms.
- **Lightweight JavaScript Libraries:** Choose libraries optimized for size and performance to minimize resource consumption on edge devices.

Example: Edge-Based Data Aggregation with JavaScript

Consider a network of environmental sensors collecting data in a remote location. You can use

Node.js and Express.js on an edge gateway to aggregate data from these sensors, perform basic processing, and then send summarized data to the cloud at longer intervals, conserving bandwidth and reducing cloud processing costs.

Combining Python and JavaScript

Python and JavaScript can be used together to create powerful edge computing solutions. Python can handle tasks like data processing and machine learning, while JavaScript can manage communication, web interfaces, and integration with other systems.

Example: Edge-Based Image Recognition

A camera captures images of products on a production line. A Python script running on an edge device uses a machine learning model to identify defective products. The results are then sent to a Node.js server running on the same device, which triggers an alert and updates a web interface accessible to operators.

Benefits of Using Python and JavaScript for Edge Computing

- **Versatility:** Both languages offer extensive libraries and frameworks for various edge computing tasks.
- **Ease of Development:** Python and JavaScript are relatively easy to learn and use, with large and active communities.
- **Cross-Platform Compatibility:** Both languages can run on various operating systems and hardware platforms, providing flexibility in your edge deployments.

By leveraging the strengths of Python and JavaScript, you can implement sophisticated edge computing functionalities in your IoT solutions, enabling real-time processing, reduced latency, and increased autonomy at the edge.

Benefits and Challenges of Edge Computing

While edge computing offers compelling advantages for IoT, it also presents its own set of challenges. This section provides a balanced perspective by exploring both the benefits and challenges of adopting edge computing in your IoT solutions.

Benefits of Edge Computing

1. **Reduced Latency:** Processing data closer to the source significantly reduces latency,

enabling real-time applications and faster response times. This is critical for applications like industrial automation, autonomous vehicles, and real-time analytics where milliseconds matter.

2. **Bandwidth Optimization:** By processing data at the edge, you reduce the amount of data that needs to be transmitted to the cloud. This conserves network bandwidth, lowers transmission costs, and improves overall network efficiency.

3. **Increased Autonomy:** Edge devices can operate independently, even with intermittent or no connectivity to the cloud. This is crucial for remote deployments, mobile IoT devices, and scenarios where continuous cloud connectivity is not feasible.

4. **Enhanced Security:** Sensitive data can be processed and analyzed locally, reducing the risk of data breaches during transmission to the cloud. This is particularly important for applications dealing with confidential information like healthcare data or financial transactions.

5. **Improved Scalability:** Edge computing distributes the processing load across multiple edge devices and servers, reducing the burden on centralized cloud resources.

This allows your IoT solution to scale more efficiently as the number of devices and data volume increases.

6. **Cost Savings:** By reducing data transmission and cloud processing needs, edge computing can lead to significant cost savings. This is especially beneficial for applications generating large volumes of data, such as video surveillance or environmental monitoring.

Challenges of Edge Computing

1. **Increased Complexity:** Managing and orchestrating a distributed network of edge devices can be more complex than managing a centralized cloud environment. This includes deploying, updating, and monitoring software and ensuring the security of edge devices.
2. **Limited Resources:** Edge devices often have limited processing power, memory, and storage compared to cloud servers. This can constrain the complexity of applications and algorithms that can be deployed at the edge.
3. **Security Concerns:** Securing edge devices can be challenging due to their distributed nature and potential physical vulnerabilities.

Implementing robust security measures, such as encryption, authentication, and access control, is crucial.

4. **Data Management:** Managing data across a distributed edge environment requires careful consideration of data synchronization, consistency, and governance. This includes ensuring data integrity, handling data conflicts, and implementing data backup and recovery strategies.

5. **Connectivity Challenges:** Edge devices may experience intermittent or unreliable connectivity, especially in remote or mobile deployments. This can affect data transmission, synchronization, and application performance.

6. **Skillset Requirements:** Implementing and managing edge computing solutions may require specialized skills in areas like embedded systems, networking, and cybersecurity.

Overcoming the Challenges

While edge computing presents challenges, there are strategies to mitigate them:

- **Edge Management Platforms:** Utilize platforms that simplify edge device management, software deployment, and monitoring.
- **Lightweight Technologies:** Employ technologies and frameworks optimized for resource-constrained edge devices.
- **Robust Security Measures:** Implement strong security protocols, encryption, and authentication mechanisms.
- **Efficient Data Management:** Utilize data synchronization and caching techniques to manage data effectively.
- **Hybrid Architectures:** Combine edge computing with cloud computing to leverage the strengths of both paradigms.

By carefully considering these benefits and challenges, and implementing appropriate strategies to address the challenges, you can effectively leverage edge computing to build more efficient, responsive, and secure IoT solutions.

Chapter XI. Advanced IoT Development

Integrating AI and Machine Learning in IoT

As we venture further into the world of IoT, we encounter the exciting realm where artificial intelligence (AI) and machine learning (ML) converge with connected devices. This chapter explores the transformative potential of integrating AI and ML into your IoT solutions, enabling intelligent automation, predictive capabilities, and data-driven decision-making.

AI and ML: The Brains Behind Intelligent IoT

AI and ML empower IoT systems to learn from data, identify patterns, and make predictions without explicit programming. This capability unlocks a new level of intelligence, allowing devices to adapt to changing conditions, optimize performance, and automate complex tasks.

Key Concepts:

- **Machine Learning:** Algorithms that enable computers to learn from data and make predictions or decisions. Common ML techniques include supervised learning (learning from labeled data), unsupervised learning (finding patterns in unlabeled data), and reinforcement learning (learning through trial[1] and error).

- **Deep Learning:** A subset of ML that uses artificial neural networks with multiple layers to extract complex features and patterns from data. Deep learning excels in tasks like image recognition, natural language processing, and time series analysis.
- **AI at the Edge:** Deploying AI and ML models directly on edge devices enables real-time processing, reduced latency, and increased autonomy. This is crucial for applications requiring immediate responses, such as autonomous vehicles and industrial automation.

Integrating AI and ML in IoT: Use Cases

- **Predictive Maintenance:** Analyze sensor data from industrial equipment to predict potential failures and schedule maintenance proactively, reducing downtime and costs.
- **Anomaly Detection:** Identify unusual patterns or outliers in data that might indicate

equipment malfunctions, security breaches, or other critical events.

- **Personalized Experiences:** Tailor user experiences based on individual preferences and behavior patterns learned from IoT data.
- **Smart Homes:** Automate lighting, temperature control, and security systems based on user habits and preferences learned through AI.
- **Precision Agriculture:** Optimize irrigation, fertilization, and pest control based on real-time sensor data and AI-powered analysis of soil conditions and crop health.
- **Healthcare:** Monitor patient health remotely, detect anomalies in vital signs, and provide personalized healthcare recommendations.

Implementing AI and ML in IoT

1. **Data Collection and Preparation:** Gather relevant data from your IoT devices and prepare it for training ML models. This may involve cleaning, transforming, and labeling the data.
2. **Model Training:** Select appropriate ML algorithms and train models using your prepared data. This often involves using

cloud platforms or powerful edge devices with sufficient processing capabilities.

3. **Model Deployment:** Deploy the trained models on edge devices, gateways, or cloud platforms, depending on the application's requirements for latency, bandwidth, and processing power.

4. **Model Monitoring and Retraining:** Continuously monitor the performance of deployed models and retrain them periodically with new data to maintain accuracy and adapt to changing conditions.

Tools and Technologies

- **Cloud Platforms:** AWS, Azure, and Google Cloud offer comprehensive AI and ML services, including pre-trained models, model training tools, and deployment platforms.
- **Edge AI Platforms:** NVIDIA Jetson and Google Coral provide hardware and software platforms for deploying AI at the edge.
- **ML Frameworks:** TensorFlow, PyTorch, and scikit-learn are popular frameworks for developing and deploying ML models.

- **Programming Languages:** Python is widely used for AI and ML development due to its extensive libraries and frameworks.

Challenges and Considerations

- **Data Quality:** The accuracy and reliability of AI and ML models depend heavily on the quality of the training data. Ensure your data is accurate, complete, and representative of real-world scenarios.
- **Model Complexity:** Complex ML models may require significant processing power and memory, which can be challenging for resource-constrained edge devices. Choose models and algorithms that are appropriate for your edge hardware.
- **Security and Privacy:** AI and ML models can be vulnerable to attacks and data breaches. Implement security measures to protect models and sensitive data.
- **Ethical Considerations:** Ensure your AI and ML applications are developed and deployed responsibly, considering potential biases, fairness, and accountability.

By integrating AI and ML into your IoT solutions, you can unlock a new level of intelligence, automation, and efficiency. These technologies empower your devices to learn, adapt, and make informed decisions, driving innovation and creating more impactful IoT applications.

Building IoT Systems with Low-Power Wide-Area Networks (LPWAN)

While traditional networks like Wi-Fi and Bluetooth are suitable for many IoT applications, there's a growing need for connectivity solutions that can cover vast distances with minimal power consumption. This is where Low-Power Wide-Area Networks (LPWAN) come into play. This section explores LPWAN technologies and how they enable long-range, energy-efficient communication for diverse IoT deployments.

LPWAN: Connecting the Unconnected

LPWAN technologies are designed to connect devices over wide areas (several kilometers) while consuming minimal power. This makes them ideal for applications where battery life is crucial, or devices are deployed in remote or hard-to-reach locations.

Key Characteristics of LPWAN:

- **Long Range:** Can cover distances of several kilometers, even in challenging environments.
- **Low Power Consumption:** Enables devices to operate for years on a single battery.
- **Low Bandwidth:** Suitable for applications with infrequent data transmission and small data payloads.
- **Low Cost:** LPWAN modules and network infrastructure are relatively inexpensive compared to traditional cellular networks.

LPWAN Technologies

Several LPWAN technologies are available, each with its own strengths and trade-offs:

- **LoRaWAN:** A long-range, low-power networking protocol based on the LoRa modulation technique. It operates in unlicensed spectrum and offers flexibility in network deployment.
- **Sigfox:** A proprietary LPWAN technology that operates in unlicensed spectrum. It provides a simple and cost-effective solution for basic data transmission.
- **NB-IoT (Narrowband IoT):** A cellular LPWAN technology standardized by 3GPP. It

leverages existing cellular infrastructure and offers good coverage and security.

- **LTE-M (LTE Cat-M1):** Another cellular LPWAN technology that provides higher bandwidth and lower latency than NB-IoT, making it suitable for applications requiring more frequent data transmission.

Building IoT Systems with LPWAN

1. **Choose the Right Technology:** Select the LPWAN technology that best suits your application's requirements for range, bandwidth, power consumption, and cost.
2. **Hardware Selection:** Choose appropriate LPWAN modules or devices that support your chosen technology.
3. **Network Connectivity:** Connect your devices to an LPWAN network, either through a public network provider or by deploying your own private network.
4. **Application Development:** Develop your IoT application, considering the constraints of LPWAN technologies, such as low bandwidth and infrequent data transmission.
5. **Data Management:** Implement data storage and processing solutions that align with the

characteristics of LPWAN data, such as infrequent updates and small payloads.

Use Cases for LPWAN in IoT

- **Smart Agriculture:** Monitor soil conditions, crop health, and livestock remotely.
- **Environmental Monitoring:** Track air quality, water levels, and other environmental parameters in remote areas.
- **Smart Cities:** Monitor parking spaces, track assets, and manage street lighting.
- **Industrial IoT:** Monitor equipment performance, track assets, and optimize supply chains.
- **Utilities:** Enable smart metering for water, gas, and electricity consumption.

Benefits of LPWAN

- **Extended Coverage:** Connect devices over long distances, even in challenging environments.
- **Prolonged Battery Life:** Minimize power consumption, enabling devices to operate for years on a single battery.

- **Cost-Effectiveness:** Reduce deployment and operational costs compared to traditional cellular networks.
- **Scalability:** Support a large number of devices within a wide geographical area.

Challenges of LPWAN

- **Limited Bandwidth:** Not suitable for applications requiring high data throughput or frequent data transmission.
- **Latency:** May experience higher latency than traditional networks, especially for long-range communication.
- **Security:** Implementing robust security measures is crucial to protect data transmitted over LPWAN.

By understanding the capabilities and limitations of LPWAN technologies, you can effectively leverage them to build IoT solutions that connect devices over vast distances with minimal power consumption, enabling new possibilities in various industries and applications.

Developing Scalable and Reliable IoT Solutions

The true potential of the Internet of Things is realized when solutions can seamlessly expand to accommodate a growing number of devices, users, and data volumes. This section delves into the principles and best practices for developing scalable and reliable IoT solutions that can adapt to evolving needs and withstand the test of time.

Scalability: Growing with Grace

Scalability in IoT refers to the ability of a system to handle increasing demands without compromising performance, reliability, or efficiency. This means that as the number of connected devices, users, and data volume grows, your IoT solution should continue to function smoothly and efficiently.

Key Considerations for Scalability:

- **Architecture:** Design a flexible and modular architecture that can accommodate growth. Microservices, distributed systems, and cloud-native approaches can enhance scalability.
- **Data Management:** Choose scalable data storage and processing solutions that can handle increasing data volumes. Cloud databases, data lakes, and distributed processing frameworks can be valuable assets.

- **Network Infrastructure:** Ensure your network infrastructure can support the growing number of connected devices and data traffic. Consider using scalable network protocols and technologies like LPWAN for long-range connectivity.
- **Communication Protocols:** Employ efficient and scalable communication protocols like MQTT to handle communication between a large number of devices.
- **Device Management:** Implement robust device management capabilities to handle the provisioning, monitoring, and updating of a growing number of devices.

Reliability: Ensuring Consistent Performance

Reliability in IoT means ensuring that your system operates consistently and predictably, even in the face of unexpected events, failures, or disruptions. This involves building fault-tolerant systems that can recover from errors and maintain data integrity.

Key Considerations for Reliability:

- **Redundancy:** Build redundancy into your system to handle failures. This can include redundant hardware, software, and network connections.

- **Fault Tolerance:** Design your system to tolerate failures and continue operating, even with degraded performance.
- **Error Handling:** Implement robust error handling mechanisms to catch and recover from errors gracefully.
- **Data Backup and Recovery:** Implement data backup and recovery strategies to protect against data loss.
- **Monitoring and Alerting:** Continuously monitor your system for potential issues and set up alerts to notify you of critical events.

Best Practices for Scalable and Reliable IoT Development

- **Start with a Scalable Architecture:** Design your system with scalability in mind from the beginning. Choose technologies and architectures that can accommodate growth.
- **Optimize Data Management:** Efficiently manage data storage, processing, and retrieval to handle increasing data volumes.
- **Prioritize Security:** Implement robust security measures to protect your system from attacks and data breaches.

- **Test Thoroughly:** Conduct rigorous testing to ensure your system can handle expected loads and recover from failures.
- **Monitor and Optimize:** Continuously monitor your system's performance and identify areas for optimization.
- **Embrace Automation:** Automate tasks like device provisioning, software updates, and data backups to improve efficiency and reduce manual effort.

Example: Scaling a Smart Agriculture System

Imagine a smart agriculture system that monitors soil moisture and controls irrigation for a small farm. To scale this system to accommodate a larger farm with more sensors and actuators, you might:

- **Adopt a microservices architecture:** Separate functionalities like data collection, processing, and control into independent services that can be scaled independently.
- **Utilize a cloud database:** Store sensor data and irrigation logs in a scalable cloud database like AWS DynamoDB or Azure Cosmos DB.
- **Implement a message queue:** Use a message queue like Kafka to handle

communication between sensors, actuators, and the control system, enabling asynchronous processing and improved scalability.

- **Deploy edge gateways:** Distribute processing and data aggregation to edge gateways to reduce the load on the central system.

By following these principles and best practices, you can develop IoT solutions that are not only functional but also scalable and reliable, ensuring they can adapt to future growth and provide consistent performance over time.

Chapter XII. Deployment and Maintenance of IoT Systems

Deploying IoT Applications to the Cloud and Edge Devices

Bringing your meticulously designed and developed IoT solution to life involves a crucial phase: deployment. This chapter focuses on the intricacies of deploying IoT applications, covering both cloud and edge deployments. We'll explore the strategies, tools, and best practices for successfully launching your IoT solution into the real world.

Deployment Strategies: Cloud vs. Edge

The choice of deployment strategy depends on your application's specific needs and constraints. Here's a breakdown of the two primary approaches:

Cloud Deployment:

- **Centralized Infrastructure:** Your IoT application's core logic and data storage reside in the cloud.
- **Scalability and Accessibility:** Cloud platforms offer excellent scalability and accessibility, allowing your application to

handle growth and be accessed from anywhere.

- **Powerful Resources:** Leverage the cloud's vast computing resources for data processing, analysis, and storage.
- **Suitable for:** Applications requiring centralized management, extensive data processing, and accessibility from various locations.

Edge Deployment:

- **Decentralized Processing:** Deploy your application's logic and processing capabilities on edge devices or gateways.
- **Reduced Latency:** Minimize latency by processing data closer to the source, enabling real-time responsiveness.
- **Bandwidth Efficiency:** Reduce data transmission to the cloud, conserving bandwidth and lowering costs.
- **Suitable for:** Applications requiring real-time processing, low latency, and operation in environments with limited or intermittent connectivity.

Hybrid Deployment:

- **Best of Both Worlds:** Combine cloud and edge deployments to leverage the strengths of both approaches.
- **Edge for Real-time Needs:** Deploy time-sensitive processing and control logic at the edge.
- **Cloud for Centralized Tasks:** Utilize the cloud for data storage, aggregation, and analysis.
- **Suitable for:** Applications requiring both real-time responsiveness and the scalability and resources of the cloud.

Deploying to the Cloud

1. **Choose a Cloud Platform:** Select a cloud provider that aligns with your needs and offers suitable IoT services (e.g., AWS IoT, Azure IoT Hub, Google Cloud IoT).
2. **Prepare Your Application:** Package your application code and dependencies into a deployable format (e.g., Docker containers, serverless functions).
3. **Provision Cloud Resources:** Create the necessary cloud resources, such as virtual machines, databases, and message queues.
4. **Deploy Your Application:** Use the cloud provider's deployment tools or services to

deploy your application to the cloud infrastructure.

5. **Configure and Connect Devices:** Configure your IoT devices to connect to the cloud platform and your deployed application.

6. **Monitor and Manage:** Utilize the cloud provider's monitoring and management tools to track your application's performance, resource usage, and health.

Deploying to Edge Devices

1. **Choose Edge Hardware:** Select appropriate edge devices or gateways that meet your application's processing, memory, and connectivity requirements.

2. **Prepare Your Application:** Optimize your application code for the resource constraints of edge devices. Consider using lightweight frameworks and libraries.

3. **Deploy Your Application:** Use tools like `scp` (secure copy) or containerization technologies (e.g., Docker) to deploy your application to edge devices.

4. **Configure and Connect Devices:** Configure edge devices to communicate with

sensors, actuators, and other systems as needed.

5. **Monitor and Manage:** Implement monitoring and management capabilities for your edge devices, including remote updates, log collection, and health checks.

Best Practices for IoT Deployment

- **Automate Deployment:** Use automation tools and scripts to streamline the deployment process and reduce manual effort.
- **Version Control:** Use version control systems (e.g., Git) to track changes to your application code and configurations.
- **Testing and Staging:** Thoroughly test your application in a staging environment before deploying to production.
- **Rollout Strategies:** Consider gradual rollout strategies (e.g., canary deployments) to minimize risks and ensure a smooth transition.
- **Monitoring and Logging:** Implement comprehensive monitoring and logging to track application performance, identify issues, and facilitate troubleshooting.

- **Security Considerations:** Prioritize security throughout the deployment process. Secure your cloud resources, edge devices, and communication channels.

By carefully planning your deployment strategy and following best practices, you can successfully launch your IoT solution, ensuring it runs smoothly, scales efficiently, and delivers on its intended purpose.

Monitoring and Maintaining IoT Systems

Deploying your IoT solution is just the beginning of its lifecycle. To ensure its continued success, ongoing monitoring and maintenance are essential. This section delves into the critical aspects of keeping your IoT system running smoothly, efficiently, and securely.

Monitoring: The Eyes and Ears of Your IoT System

Monitoring provides real-time visibility into the health, performance, and security of your IoT system. It allows you to track key metrics, identify potential issues, and proactively address them before they escalate into major problems.

Key Aspects of IoT Monitoring:

- **Device Monitoring:** Track the status, health, and performance of individual devices. Monitor metrics like battery life, connectivity strength, sensor readings, and error rates.
- **Network Monitoring:** Monitor the performance and availability of your network infrastructure. Track metrics like bandwidth usage, latency, packet loss, and connection stability.
- **Application Monitoring:** Monitor the performance and health of your IoT application. Track metrics like response times, error rates, resource usage, and user activity.
- **Security Monitoring:** Monitor your system for security threats and vulnerabilities. Track events like unauthorized access attempts, suspicious activity, and data breaches.
- **Data Monitoring:** Monitor the quality and integrity of your IoT data. Track metrics like data completeness, accuracy, and consistency.

Tools and Techniques for Monitoring

- **Monitoring Platforms:** Utilize cloud-based or on-premises monitoring platforms that provide dashboards, alerts, and reporting capabilities.
- **Logging:** Collect and analyze logs from devices, applications, and network components to identify issues and track events.
- **Metrics and KPIs:** Define key performance indicators (KPIs) and track relevant metrics to assess the health and efficiency of your system.
- **Alerting:** Set up alerts to notify you of critical events, such as device failures, network outages, or security breaches.
- **Visualization:** Use visualizations like charts and graphs to gain insights into your system's performance and identify trends.

Maintenance: Keeping Your System Healthy

Maintenance involves proactive and reactive measures to ensure the continued operation and optimal performance of your IoT system. This includes tasks like software updates, security patching, hardware repairs, and data management.

Key Aspects of IoT Maintenance:

- **Software Updates:** Regularly update device firmware, application software, and operating systems to patch vulnerabilities, improve performance, and add new features.
- **Security Patching:** Promptly apply security patches to address known vulnerabilities and protect your system from attacks.
- **Hardware Maintenance:** Perform regular maintenance on hardware components, such as cleaning sensors, replacing batteries, and repairing or replacing faulty devices.
- **Data Management:** Manage data storage, backups, and archiving to ensure data integrity and availability.
- **Troubleshooting and Repair:** Diagnose and resolve issues that arise, such as device failures, network connectivity problems, or application errors.

Best Practices for IoT Maintenance

- **Proactive Maintenance:** Implement preventive maintenance schedules to address potential issues before they impact system performance.
- **Remote Management:** Utilize remote management tools to perform updates,

diagnostics, and troubleshooting without physical access to devices.

- **Automation:** Automate tasks like software updates, data backups, and security patching to improve efficiency and reduce manual effort.
- **Documentation:** Maintain comprehensive documentation of your system's architecture, configurations, and maintenance procedures.
- **Testing:** Regularly test your system's functionality and performance to identify and address potential issues.

Example: Maintaining a Smart Home System

Imagine a smart home system with connected lights, thermostats, and security cameras. Maintenance tasks might include:

- **Updating firmware:** Regularly update the firmware of devices like smart bulbs and thermostats to address security vulnerabilities and improve functionality.
- **Checking battery life:** Monitor the battery life of sensors and replace batteries as needed.

- **Cleaning camera lenses:** Periodically clean the lenses of security cameras to ensure clear images.
- **Troubleshooting connectivity:** Diagnose and resolve any connectivity issues between devices and the home network.

By implementing a robust monitoring and maintenance strategy, you can ensure the longevity, efficiency, and security of your IoT system. This proactive approach minimizes downtime, optimizes performance, and maximizes the value of your connected devices.

Troubleshooting and Debugging IoT Applications

Even with meticulous planning and development, issues can arise in any IoT system. This section equips you with the knowledge and techniques for troubleshooting and debugging your IoT applications, enabling you to identify, diagnose, and resolve problems effectively.

Common Challenges in IoT Applications

IoT systems, with their intricate interplay of hardware, software, and networks, can present unique challenges when it comes to troubleshooting. Some common issues include:

- **Connectivity Problems:** Network disruptions, signal interference, or incorrect network configurations can lead to connectivity issues between devices, gateways, and the cloud.
- **Hardware Failures:** Sensor malfunctions, faulty actuators, or power supply issues can cause unexpected behavior or complete system failures.
- **Software Bugs:** Errors in application code, firmware, or device drivers can lead to unexpected behavior, data corruption, or system crashes.
- **Data Inconsistencies:** Data synchronization problems, data corruption, or incorrect data processing can lead to inaccurate readings or misleading insights.
- **Security Breaches:** Vulnerabilities in devices, software, or networks can expose your system to unauthorized access, data breaches, or malicious attacks.

Troubleshooting Techniques

1. **Identify the Problem:** Gather information about the issue, including error messages, logs, and user reports. Observe the system's behavior and try to pinpoint the source of the problem.
2. **Isolate the Cause:** Use techniques like divide and conquer to isolate the faulty component or subsystem. This might involve disconnecting devices, testing individual components, or analyzing logs to narrow down the source of the error.
3. **Diagnose the Issue:** Once you've isolated the cause, use debugging tools and techniques to diagnose the specific problem. This might involve examining code, analyzing data flow, or using network diagnostic tools.
4. **Implement a Solution:** Based on your diagnosis, implement a solution to address the issue. This might involve fixing code, replacing hardware, updating firmware, or reconfiguring network settings.
5. **Test and Verify:** After implementing a solution, thoroughly test the system to ensure the problem is resolved and that the solution hasn't introduced new issues.

Debugging Tools and Techniques

- **Debuggers:** Use debuggers to step through code, inspect variables, and identify the source of errors.
- **Logging:** Utilize logging to record events, errors, and data flow, providing valuable insights into the system's behavior.
- **Network Analyzers:** Use network analyzers (e.g., Wireshark) to capture and analyze network traffic, identifying connectivity issues or security breaches.
- **Simulators and Emulators:** Use simulators or emulators to test your application in a controlled environment, replicating real-world scenarios.
- **Remote Diagnostics:** Implement remote diagnostics capabilities to access device logs, monitor performance, and perform troubleshooting remotely.

Best Practices for Troubleshooting

- **Start with the Obvious:** Check for simple issues like loose connections, power supply problems, or incorrect configurations before diving into complex debugging.
- **Document Everything:** Keep detailed records of your troubleshooting steps, findings, and solutions. This documentation

can be invaluable for future debugging efforts.

- **Seek Help When Needed:** Don't hesitate to seek help from online communities, forums, or technical support if you encounter challenging problems.
- **Learn from Mistakes:** Analyze the root causes of issues and implement preventive measures to avoid similar problems in the future.

Example: Troubleshooting Connectivity Issues

Imagine a smart agriculture system where sensors are intermittently losing connection to the gateway. Troubleshooting steps might include:

1. **Check Physical Connections:** Ensure sensors are properly connected to the gateway and that there are no loose wires or damaged connectors.
2. **Analyze Signal Strength:** Use network diagnostic tools to assess the signal strength between sensors and the gateway. Identify potential sources of interference or weak signal areas.
3. **Verify Network Configuration:** Check the network settings on both sensors and the

gateway to ensure they are correctly configured for the same network.

4. **Examine Logs:** Analyze logs from the gateway and sensors to identify any error messages or patterns related to connectivity issues.

5. **Consider Environmental Factors:** Assess environmental factors that might be affecting connectivity, such as distance, obstacles, or weather conditions.

By systematically applying these troubleshooting and debugging techniques, you can effectively address issues that arise in your IoT applications, ensuring their continued operation and optimal performance.

CONCLUSION

As we reach the end of this exploration into the world of IoT development with Python and JavaScript, you stand equipped with a powerful toolkit of knowledge and skills. You've delved into the core concepts of IoT, mastered essential hardware and software tools, and learned to build real-world applications that bridge the gap between the physical and digital realms.

This book has provided a comprehensive foundation, but the journey of learning and innovation in IoT is ongoing. The field is constantly evolving, with new technologies, protocols, and applications emerging at a rapid pace. As you continue your journey, remember to stay curious, embrace experimentation, and remain adaptable to the ever-changing landscape of IoT.

Key Takeaways

Throughout this book, we've emphasized several key principles that are crucial for successful IoT development:

- **Security:** Prioritize security at every stage of the development process, from device selection to data management and communication. Protecting your IoT systems from threats and vulnerabilities is paramount to ensuring their integrity and reliability.
- **Scalability:** Design your solutions with scalability in mind, choosing technologies and architectures that can accommodate growth and adapt to evolving needs.
- **Reliability:** Build robust and fault-tolerant systems that can withstand disruptions and maintain consistent performance.
- **Efficiency:** Optimize your applications for resource-constrained environments, especially when deploying to edge devices. Choose efficient algorithms, minimize power consumption, and utilize appropriate communication protocols.
- **Data-Driven Decision Making:** Leverage the power of data analytics and visualization to extract meaningful insights from your IoT

data, driving informed decisions and optimizing system performance.
- **Ethical Considerations:** Develop and deploy IoT solutions responsibly, considering potential ethical implications, privacy concerns, and societal impact.

The Future of IoT

The Internet of Things is poised to transform every aspect of our lives, from how we live and work to how we interact with the world around us. As IoT technologies continue to advance, we can expect even more innovative and impactful applications to emerge, addressing challenges in areas like healthcare, agriculture, transportation, and environmental sustainability.

Your Role in Shaping the Future

As an IoT developer, you have a crucial role to play in shaping this future. By combining your creativity, technical skills, and ethical awareness, you can contribute to building a world where technology seamlessly integrates with our lives, enhancing efficiency, sustainability, and overall well-being.

Thank you for joining me on this exploration of IoT development with Python and JavaScript. We hope this book has empowered you to embark on your own IoT adventures and contribute to the exciting future of connected things.